D1357177

CLIFFORD PARKER

365 Things to Know

illustrated by
Cathi · Tony Chatfield · Esmé Eve
Kenneth Ody · Porter G · Michael Shoebridge

HAMLYN
LONDON · NEW YORK · SYDNEY · TORONTO

1ST JANUARY

What is the meaning of January?

The first month is the gateway to the New Year, and takes its name from Janus, a two-headed Roman god who guarded doors and gates. One of his heads was said to look towards the past, the other to the future.

When the Romans first borrowed their calendar from the Greeks, they had a year only 304 days long and divided into ten months, beginning with March.

Legend has it that January and February were added by a King of Rome called Numa Pompilius in about 700 B.C. He made January the eleventh month and February the twelfth.

This calendar, though more accurate than the old one, was still not good enough. By the time of Julius Caesar, the dates were three months ahead of the seasons. So, in 46 B.C. Caesar ordered that the calendar be brought up to date, and in doing so made January the first month and February the second. Caesar's Calendar, called the Julian Calendar, was used for 1,500 years.

January 1st, New Year's Day, is celebrated as a holiday in many countries. The Scottish *Hogmanay* is famous all over the world, and the custom of letting in the New Year by joining hands at midnight to sing *Auld Lang Syne* is observed in Britain and many other English-speaking countries. New Year's Day is a great time for family parties and reunions, and a time for New Year Resolutions — not all of which, however, are kept for very long!

In the big cities of the world, many people gather in a main square to welcome the New Year. In London, Trafalgar Square is the traditional gathering place, while New Yorkers crowd into Times Square. In Japan, New Year celebrations go on for three days. In India, January 1st is a public holiday.

Of the New Year customs which have survived in Britain, perhaps the most common is that of 'first-footing', when people go from house to house to wish their friends happiness in the New Year. A dark man as the first caller is held to be very lucky, especially if he carries a piece of coal and a slice of bread, to ensure food and warmth in the months to come.

Can a penguin fly?

No — though many thousands of years ago his ancestors could. Then they took to living by the sea and spending a lot of time in the water. They learned to use their wings, as well as their feet, for swimming. Over many, many years the wings changed their shape and the feathers grew smaller, leaving the penguin with two limbs, which made excellent paddles, but which were useless for flying. Today, if a penguin were to be given a pair of large wings he would still be unable to fly: the shape of his whole body has changed to suit his life in the sea. In any case, he is now much too heavy to fly.

What are Aesop's Fables?

Long ago, in Ancient Greece, there lived a slave called Aesop. He seems to have been an ugly little man, but people liked him because he told such amusing stories; they were 'fables', or stories with a moral.

Aesop was a very observant man, who noticed other people's faults, and wove them into his stories, often making the people themselves into animals. When his master, King Croesus, sent him with some money to Delphi, for instance, the greedy people asked for more, and Aesop told them the story of the *Man who Killed the Goose who laid the Golden Eggs*. The boy who cried 'Wolf!', the Hare and the Tortoise, the Grasshopper and the Ant, and the Fox who said 'Sour Grapes!' are more world-famous characters from Aesop's fables.

5

Why do some things float?

Anything lighter than water floats upon it: anything heavier sinks to the bottom. An object lighter than water presses down on the surface until it has pushed away its own weight of water; it then stops sinking because it has no more weight to press down with. Any object heavier than water pushes away its own volume, or space, of water, is still left with some weight to press down with, and so sinks to the bottom.

Cork, which is the bark of the cork oak, grown mainly in Spain, is extremely light and so floats better than most other materials. For this reason it is used in the making of lifebelts and safety jackets.

4TH JANUARY

Are whales fish?

No. Whales are mammals, just as we are. They certainly *look* like fish, and spend all their lives in the sea, but long, long ago they were land animals. They probably took to the sea in search of food, or because fiercer animals drove them there. Their shape changed over the course of time, just as did the shapes of the penguins and seals, to make them better suited to life in the water. Unlike fish, whales are warm-blooded. To keep out the cold they have a thick layer of fat, called blubber, all over their bodies. They have lungs, not gills, and breathe air just as land animals do. Their young are born alive, not hatched from eggs. Whales are divided into two kinds: the toothed whales — which include the sperm whale, the dolphin, the porpoise and the narwhal — and the whalebone whales, which are the rorquals and the right whales. The whalebone whales have, instead of teeth, a huge, gristly sieve, through which they strain the seawater to trap the tiny animals on which they feed.

Why is fire hot?

When a thing burns, the substances from which it is made are broken down with the oxygen gas in the air to form other substances. In a coal fire, for instance, it is mainly the carbon in the coal which unites with the oxygen. The breaking down of the substances in this chemical action releases some of the energy locked away in them. This energy is heat. It is given off in the form of waves, just as light is transmitted as waves, but we feel them instead of seeing them.

Heat reaches us in three ways: by convection, conduction and radiation.

Convection is when the air nearest the fire is warmed, and flows around the room.

Conduction is the moving of heat, by its own power, through an object. The heat you feel when you put your hand on the surround of a fireplace is conducted heat.

Radiant heat is made of waves which move through the air until they strike a solid object. If you are sitting opposite the fire the object is you, and the waves are making you warm by their direct action on your skin.

Why is the sky blue?

Our earth is wrapped in a blanket of gas called the *atmosphere*. The atmosphere, which is the air we breathe, is made up of gases like oxygen, nitrogen, carbon dioxide, water vapour and tiny specks of floating dust.

When sunlight hits this layer, the gases split up the white light into its different colours. Of these different colours — red, orange, yellow, green, blue, indigo and violet — the blue is spread about the most and so appears to fill the sky.

Where there is no atmosphere, as on the moon, the sky appears to be black. Though the surface of the moon may be brightly lit, there is no gas around it to break up the passing sunlight into colours. The black sky, with all the stars and planets shining brightly, is what the astronauts see when their craft leave the earth's layer of gas and move into the vacuum of outer space.

How fast can a pigeon fly?

A homing, or racing, pigeon flies at a speed of about 40 miles an hour, sometimes more, sometimes less, depending on the distance and the direction of the wind. Pigeon races can be over distances of from fifty to seven hundred miles. The pigeons are sent away in baskets — you can often see them on railway stations — and are released together at a fixed time. They have a special instinct which guides each one right back to its own loft, where the owner times its arrival. At one time pigeons were used to carry messages, but the telephone and telegraph do this for us today. Pigeon racing is now a popular sport.

8TH JANUARY

What is porcelain?

Your mother's best tea-service may well be porcelain. It is a form of fine pottery discovered and perfected long ago by the Chinese. It reached Europe about four hundred years ago, but the first European attempts at making it were not very good until the secret of the special clay needed for it was discovered at Dresden, Germany, in 1708. True porcelain is made from kaolin, or china clay. It is very hard and strong, but so fine that light can be seen through it. It is from the name of the clay that we get our word 'china' to describe fine pottery. As well as being made into cups and saucers, porcelain is also made into delicate little statues and ornaments. The most famous Chinese porcelain is that of the Ming Dynasty (1368—1644). The most famous European porcelain is that produced at Dresden and in Sèvres, France.

8

Can we have light without heat?

The kinds of light we are most familiar with — daylight, firelight, electric light — are all accompanied by heat. But there are other forms of light which are created by chemical action, and which are cold.

One such kind of light is called *luminescence* and is produced by certain insects, such as the glow-worm and firefly, as well as by some fishes and other sea creatures.

Another kind of cold light is called *phosphorescence* and is produced by certain chemical substances after they have been exposed to daylight. Calcium sulphide, for instance, glows in the dark after being allowed to 'soak' up light during the daytime.

Why does a horse have only one toe on each foot?

Many years ago, long before man appeared on earth, lived a little animal called Eohippus. Eohippus was about the size of a dog and had four toes on its front feet and three on the back. It is from Eohippus that

horses, donkeys and zebras are descended. Because it was a gentle creature, eating only grass, it was hunted by the fierce, meat-eating animals, and to escape them it had to rely on its fleetness of foot. After many generations of running, its descendants' feet changed shape. The toenails grew hard and strong. Then the middle toe on each foot grew bigger and stronger than the others until in the end only this toe was used for running on. The other toes became smaller and smaller through lack of use until they disappeared from sight altogether, though traces of them remain today in the 'splint' bones of the horse's leg. The hooves, of course, are the nails of the middle toes, beautifully shaped by nature to carry their owners surely and swiftly.

How can you tell butterflies from moths?

Butterflies and moths together make up the great order of insects known as *Lepidoptera*. There are several main points of difference. Butterflies generally come out during the day, rest with their wings pointing upwards and have club-like tips to their *antennae*, or feelers. Moths generally come out at night, are less brightly coloured than butterflies, and rest with their wings folded flat across their bodies. Their antennae do not end in little knobs, but instead are often branched or feathery.

What was the art of the cavemen?

Our Stone Age ancestors have left many paintings which tell us much about the animals which were living at the time. The cavemen lived by hunting and believed strongly in magic. To bring them success in the hunt they painted the walls of caves with pictures of the animals they hoped to kill. These caves were used for religious rites before the chase. In Europe more than a hundred such caves have been discovered

10

with the paintings still brightly-coloured, preserved by the darkness and the damp. The most famous of these caves is that at Lascaux, in France, discovered in 1940 by some adventurous boys looking for their dog.

The cavemen used flint chisels to carve outlines in the limestone walls, and then coloured in the outlines with natural dyes mixed with animal fat. Sometimes they painted complete hunting scenes, showing animals being chased and struck by spears. Sometimes, too, they made holes in the painted rock with real spears, perhaps in the excitement of a religious dance.

14TH JANUARY

What is an opera?

Opera is a mixture of music and acting, and gets its name from the Italian *opera in musica* (a musical work). The story of the opera is told in song, usually in the language in which it was first written, and this can make it difficult to follow. Despite this, however, an opera is a very beautiful thing to see and hear.

Opera began in Florence, in Italy, about 1582, when people were trying to revive Greek drama, which had music as well as words. The first opera we know about was called *Dafne*, but most of the music for this has been lost. However, one called *Orfeo*, written in 1607 by Monteverdi, is still performed today. The first opera house was opened in Venice in 1637.

Opera spread from Italy to France and Germany, and the operas performed today have been written by people from all over the world. Some famous composers are: Rossini, Verdi, Puccini (Italian); Mozart (Italian and German); Wagner (German); Gounod and Bizet (French); Glinka, Tchaikovsky, Borodin, Rimsky-Korsakov (Russian).

What is a fresco?

A fresco is a special kind of wall-painting done on wet plaster, so that the colouring soaks well into the surface of the wall. Because the plaster has to be fresh — 'fresco' is Italian for 'fresh' — the artist first draws his design on a large sheet of paper and then copies it, piece by piece, as the plaster is applied to the wall.

Frescoes were the favourite method of wall decoration before the introduction of oil paints. They will only last, however, in hot dry countries such as Italy. A damp climate would soon ruin them.

The art of the fresco is an ancient one. For instance, we know much about life in Crete, 1,500 years before Christ, from frescoes found at Knossos. But the finest frescoes of all are those made in Italy in Renaissance times. Perhaps the best of these are those by Michelangelo on the ceiling of the Sistine Chapel in the Vatican.

Which Greek city is named after a goddess?

Athens, the capital city of Greece, is named after Athene, or Athena, a daughter of Zeus. The goddess of wisdom, she was also the goddess of war, the sciences and the arts. It was believed that she would protect a city named after her. One of the most famous old buildings in Athens, the Parthenon, was built as a temple in her honour and takes its name from her title of 'Parthenos' or 'maiden'.

What is sand made of?

Sand is a collection of countless millions of tiny pieces of rock, broken off by the action of wind, rain, frost or water. The rubbing together of these pieces wears them down into the tiny grains you see on the seashore. The minerals which make up sand are mainly quartz, mica and felspar. We use sand in the making of bricks, mortar and cement; for polishing and cleaning other materials, and for lightening heavy soils.

Who were the Aztecs?

The Aztecs — their name means *crane people* — were a tribe of American Indians who lived in Mexico at the time of the Spanish conquest in the early sixteenth century. They were a proud, warlike people, who subdued the tribes around them and exacted from them tributes of cotton, gold and other goods.

The rise of the Aztecs really began about 1325, when they captured and fortified an island in Lake Tenochtitlan, now the site of Mexico City. From here they sent out armies to conquer the other tribes until, by the time they were themselves overthrown by the Spanish soldiers of Cortes, their rule stretched across Mexico from the Atlantic to the Pacific.

Cortes and his Spanish troops were helped by other Indian tribes to fight the Aztecs: not surprisingly, for the sun-worship of the Aztecs demanded many human sacrifices, and these were captured from the tribes round about. Cortes overthrew the Aztec rulers, Montezuma II and Cuauhtemoc, ransacked the capital and destroyed the organisation of the empire. In many ways it was a pity, because, cruel though the Aztecs were, their civilisation had produced many fine things: they had great skill in building, carving, pottery, painting, and made great discoveries in medicine and farming.

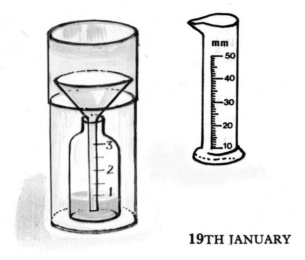

How did the piano get its name?

The piano was an Italian invention and, naturally, carries an Italian name. Its full name is *pianoforte*, from the Italian *piano e forte*, which means 'soft and loud'. The mechanism of earlier keyboard instruments, like the harpsichord and spinet, *plucked* the strings. The clavichord had strikers which *struck* the strings, but stayed in contact with them. The strikers of a piano hit the strings, and immediately bounce off.

When a pianist hits a key, the mechanism inside the piano jerks a hammer towards the strings of that particular note. (Most of the notes are made by three strings, the rest by two.) On hitting the strings, the hammer immediately bounces away and a device called a *damper* presses on the strings and silences them. If the pianist holds his finger on the key, however, the damper is held

19TH JANUARY

How is rainfall measured?

Rainfall is measured with a simple piece of equipment called a rain gauge. It consists of a wide-mouthed funnel which stands in a collecting-jar. The rain falls into the funnel and runs down into the jar. At certain intervals, the water in the jar is poured into a measuring-glass, which is marked off in inches or centimetres, and the amount measured. This is how, after a bad storm, you can be told on the radio or television that so many centimetres of rain have fallen in so many hours.

off and the note continues until the key is released.

The piano also has two foot pedals. One of them, when pressed, makes each hammer strike one string fewer, so producing less tone. The other lifts the damper mechanism away from the strings, allowing all the notes to sound very loudly and to run into one another. So, you see, the name 'soft and loud' is a very fitting one.

21ST JANUARY

Who first discovered America?

In fourteen hundred and ninety-two,
Columbus sailed the ocean blue.
You have perhaps learned that rhyme at school to help you remember the date of Christopher Columbus's 'discovery' of America. But almost five hundred years before Columbus's voyage, Vikings landed from their colonies in Iceland and Greenland and began to farm the rich soil of a part of America they called 'Vinland'.

The Vikings' discovery of America was made, like so many others, by accident. In the year A.D. 986, a merchant named Bjarni Herjolfsson was sailing from Iceland to Greenland when he was blown off course and sighted unknown lands far to the west. Eventually, he returned to tell the tale and, round about the year A.D. 1,000, he sold his ship to Leif Ericsson, known as Leif the Lucky.

Leif and his crew sailed to the land Bjarni had told them about, and found it unlike any other they had ever seen, so rich was it in animals and plants, so warm that even in winter there was hardly a frost. Leif named it Vinland, or 'Wineland', because of the many wild grapevines which grew there. More expeditions followed and the Vikings settled down in the land they now looked upon as home. They possibly stayed there until the fifteenth century, but nobody knows. Nobody knows, either, exactly where Vinland was. It had certainly been forgotten by 1492, when Christopher Columbus discovered the Bahamas. He never found the mainland.

15

Why were castles built?

22ND JANUARY

Why is the thistle the emblem of Scotland?

In the eighth century an army of invading Danes was moving up at night to attack Stirling Castle, the ancient home of the Scottish kings. The Scots inside the castle had no idea that the enemy was approaching until one of the barefooted Danish scouts trod on a thistle and let out a great yell. Warned of their danger, the Scots poured out of the castle, defeated the Danes, and afterwards adopted the thistle as their emblem.

The thistle is also the badge of the Order of the Thistle, a Scottish order of knighthood which dates from 1687.

From prehistoric times until the use of gunpowder became common, castles were built for defence. The earliest castles were simply earthworks: an example of this is the prehistoric Maiden Castle in Dorset. The Romans built castles as they advanced through Europe, choosing a patch of ground on the top of a hill and surrounding it with a ditch and sometimes a timber palisade. (The word 'castle' actually comes from the Roman *castellum*, meaning 'fort'.)

The Normans built many castles in England to impose their rule on the Saxons after the Conquest. At first, these castles were of wood, but were later built of stone. During the Middle Ages, castles grew bigger and more complicated, with several walls enclosing one another and towers from which attackers could be fired upon from all directions. At the advance of enemy forces,

How many stars are there?

Nobody knows how many stars there are. One reason is that we cannot see all of them, even with the most powerful telescope. The earth we live on is just a tiny little planet, not a star. The earth goes round and round a medium-sized star — the sun. The sun, in its turn, is only one of thousands of millions of stars in a collection, or galaxy, called the Milky Way. And the Milky Way is only one of the many millions of galaxies in space, even though it is so big that light takes a hundred thousand years to cross from one side of it to the other. So it seems unlikely that we shall ever be able to count all the stars. Even if we could, the numbers would be so great that most people would be unable to imagine them.

villagers living nearby would seek the protection of the castle and its soldiers, taking their animals and supplies with them, so that there would be enough food to last out a siege.

Castles suddenly became useless with the coming of gunpowder, which meant that attackers could batter down the walls with big guns from a safe distance. From the end of the fifteenth century, no more castles were built for defence in England. During the Civil War (1642—1649), however, some proved strong enough to stand up to bombardment by Roundhead cannon. Oliver Cromwell pulled down several castles which had been used against him. However, there are still many castles standing throughout Europe, which, when their military use was over, were used simply as homes by their noble owners.

17

What was the Children's Crusade?

Between 1100 and 1300 the Christian rulers of Europe organised several expeditions, or crusades, to Palestine with the object of recovering the Holy Places from the Saracens. In 1212 happened the strangest and most tragic crusade of them all: the Children's Crusade. A twelve-year-old shepherd boy named Stephen went to the King of France with a letter which he said came from Christ, and asked him to start a crusade. The King would not, so Stephen announced that he would organise a crusade of children, and that the sea would miraculously dry up to allow them to walk to the Holy Land.

Stephen set off and soon collected thirty thousand children. Many of them died from hunger and thirst on the march through France to the sea — a hot summer that year had brought drought to the land. When the survivors reached Marseilles, the port on the Mediterranean, they found that the sea would not dry up to let them cross. Two rascally merchants took them aboard seven ships, promising to take them to Palestine, but their real intention was to sell them into slavery. Two of the ships were wrecked in a storm. The rest reached Algeria, where the children were duly sold. Of the thirty thousand children who set off, only one ever got back to France, and that was after eighteen years of slavery.

At the same time as the French Children's Crusade got under way, another one was started in Germany by a boy called Nicolas. Twenty thousand children set off on this: only one in ten finally returned home.

Why do animals have tails?

Animals' tails have been adapted in different ways for many different uses. Monkeys use their long tails for grasping, almost as an extra hand. Beavers have flat tails which they use to pat down the mud coverings of their lodges, and for thumping the water to warn of the approach of an enemy. Crocodiles use their armoured tails for swimming, and also to knock other animals into the water where they can be seized and eaten. The squirrel uses its tail as a balancer as it leaps through the trees. Horses and cattle use their tails to whisk flies away.

What is smoke?

Kangaroos use them for balancing during their great leaps, and as a stool when they sit back for a rest. Birds use their tails as brakes and rudders in flight. The male peacock and the lyre bird use their large and gaudy tails to attract a mate. A rabbit's tiny tail does not, at first glance, seem to be much use — but the mother's white 'scut' guides the young to safety when the family flees from one of its many enemies.

When a fire burns, it gives off a vapour, or gas, which carries with it millions of small pieces of solid matter. This mixture of gas and little pieces of solids is smoke. The gas is invisible: what you see is the cloud of tiny 'grains' carried with it. Smoke is the result of incomplete burning: if it is passed through a very hot furnace the little pieces of solid matter are burned up and only gas is left. What the solid pieces are depends on what is being burned: smoke from coal contains mainly carbon particles. Smoke is a problem in many of our big cities and an Act of Parliament — the Smoke Abatement Act — has been passed to make people more careful about what they let out from their home and factory chimneys. Many cities have smoke-free zones, where it is forbidden to burn anything which will foul the air.

What are lungs?

Lungs are the organs through which we, and most other land animals, breathe. We have two lungs, carried in the chest. A branch of the windpipe goes to each one. When we breathe in, the lungs expand and suck in air. The air travels through tubes in the lungs which divide many times, getting smaller and smaller. Finally it reaches thousands of little spaces, or sacs, in which our blood takes from it the oxygen it needs to keep our bodies working. At the same time as it takes the oxygen, the blood gets rid of the carbon dioxide, a waste gas which the body does not want. This carbon dioxide is what we breathe out.

We can see how lungs came into being by studying a peculiar fish called the lungfish. The lungfish has both gills and a lung for breathing with. In the hot countries in which it lives, the pools which are its home dry up for part of the year. When this happens, it buries itself in the mud and breathes through its lung, which is really a modified swimming bladder.

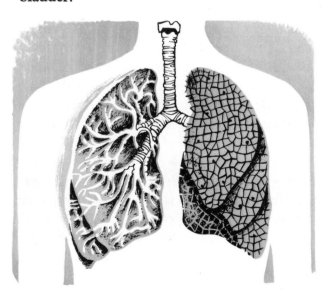

What is the Vatican?

For more than a thousand years the Roman Catholic Church ruled a large section of central Italy, including Rome itself, known as the Papal States. In 1870 the Papal States were taken over by the King of Italy, leaving only a small area inside Rome, known as the Vatican City, to be ruled over by the Church.

The Vatican is really a country in its own right. Almost a thousand people live within its walls. It has its own stamps, its own flag, its own railway station, and is governed by a special council appointed by the Pope, the head of the Roman Catholic Church.

Inside the one-sixth of a square mile of the Vatican are many fine buildings and priceless works of art. The Vatican Palace, in which the Pope lives, is a collection of buildings and open courts covering five hectares and having more than a thousand rooms. One of the Palace buildings is the Sistine Chapel, whose walls and ceilings are decorated with paintings by great artists of the Renaissance, most notably Michelangelo.

The Vatican Museum holds a great many

famous statues and paintings. Some of the rooms were decorated by Raphael. Among the many great artists whose paintings hang in the museum are Titian and Leonardo da Vinci.

The Vatican Library holds many ancient manuscripts and early printed books.

Next to the Palace is St Peter's Basilica, the largest Christian church in the world. It was begun in 1506 by Pope Julius II, on the site of an earlier church, over a crypt in which the body of St Peter was believed to lie. Michelangelo played a great part in the building of St Peter's, and himself designed the great dome.

Michelangelo also designed the colourful uniforms worn by the Swiss Guards who protect the Pope in his Palace. When on duty the famous Guards carry halberds, a kind of long spear with an axe-head fitted near the top.

30TH JANUARY

Which English king was beheaded?

Charles I came to the throne of England in 1625, and for the whole of his reign was involved in quarrel after quarrel with Parliament, usually about money. In January 1642 Charles attempted to arrest five members of the Parliament, failed, and had to leave London. In August the first Civil War began, and ended in 1645 with the Battle of Naseby. Charles was taken prisoner, but war broke out again, and Parliament thought the only way to make peace was to kill the king. So Charles was tried for treason, and, in January, 1649, he was beheaded.

21

How does a camera take a photograph?

1. Your camera.

FILM

LENS

2. You take a photograph.

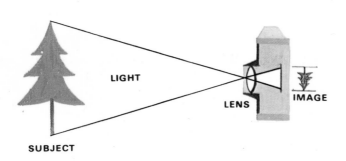

LIGHT

LENS

IMAGE

SUBJECT

When you press the button on your camera, the shutter is opened for a fraction of a second, and the picture of the subject you are photographing is exposed on to the film.

3. The negative is made.

The film is a very sensitive piece of celluloid. When it is put through a chemical known as a 'developer', an image appears on it, but the dark parts appear light and the light parts dark. This is called a 'negative'. The film must be developed in near-darkness, a stronger light would smudge the image.

4. The positive is printed.

LIGHT

NEGATIVE

POSITIVE

The negative is then placed on to a piece of sensitive coated paper. These are exposed together to a strong light, and a further image is formed, but this time, because of the special coating, where the light hits the paper it becomes dark, but the light cannot penetrate the dark parts of the negative, so the paper underneath them appears light. The paper now holds a 'positive' image.

5. You have a photograph.

The paper is now put into another developer. When the image is dark enough, it is put into a 'fix', which stops further chemical change. It is then washed and dried, and you have a photograph.

What is the meaning of February?

We discovered earlier how Julius Caesar made February the second month instead of the twelfth. Until Caesar's time, February had thirty days. Caesar took one day to add to July, the month named after him. Then Augustus took another one to add to August, the month named after *him,* leaving February with only twenty-eight days. February does, however, have an extra day every four years — every *Leap Year* — to keep the calendar exactly in time with the seasons.

The name comes from the Latin *Februarius,* meaning 'to purify'. The ancient Romans held a festival of purification to prepare for the year to come, and the name stuck to the month even after it was moved from twelfth to second in the calendar.

What is a cave?

A cave is a hollow place underground and is generally formed in one of two ways: either by water trickling down from the surface and dissolving the underground rock, or by the action of waves on the seashore.

The first kind of cave is formed among rocks such as chalk or limestone, which are affected by acids. It is really the acid in the water, and not the water itself, which dissolves the rock. This acid, and it is only a little, is picked up by the water as it seeps through peaty soil on its way underground.

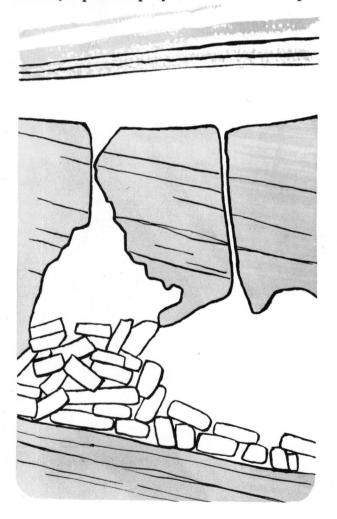

Caves on the seashore are formed by the constant battering of the waves. After long years of this, a piece of rock will break away at a weak point. This will keep on happening until quite a big hole is made.

We have already mentioned the fact that, long ago, many people lived in caves. In certain parts of the world, some still do. Caves are also homes for many animals, from insects, birds and bats to tigers, bears and wolves.

The exploration of caves is very interesting and exciting, but sometimes dangerous. There are many clubs in Britain and overseas for those who want to go caving and pot-holing.

What is a geyser?

A geyser is a hot spring which, every so often, throws a great spout of boiling water and steam high into the air.

The spouting happens because the rocks over which the water flows underground are hot, so hot that the water boils and turns into steam. At regular intervals a great mass of steam builds up and thrusts the water on top of it out to the surface.

Geysers are found in countries where there are, or were, volcanoes. Most of them are found in Iceland, New Zealand and the United States. The word 'geyser' itself is an Icelandic one.

Geyser is also the name given to a piece of equipment which can heat up water very quickly (you may have one in your kitchen). The water runs through a long coil of metal piping — usually copper — which is heated all along its length. It enters the pipe cold, but gets hot in the time it takes to come out at the other end.

4TH FEBRUARY

Who was the Iron Chancellor?

A hundred years ago, Germany was divided into many small states, or countries. In one of these states, Prussia, the chancellor, or chief minister to the king, was Otto von Bismarck. A strong and ruthless man, Bismarck built up Prussia into the strongest of all the German states and made its army feared throughout Europe. When the states were gathered into one Empire in 1871, Bismarck, now a prince, and his king, now an emperor, were at their head. Prince Bismarck continued to make the new empire stronger until he was dismissed by a new emperor in 1890. He got his nickname of 'The Iron Chancellor' when he said that Germany could only become a great power 'through blood and iron'.

25

How does skin breathe?

You may have noticed that your mother does not like you to wear a plastic mackintosh or rubber boots for too long because, she says, they do not let your skin 'breathe'. Although your skin does not actually breathe, your mother is being very wise. For skin has a certain job to do for which it must have air circulating around it, and materials like plastic and rubber prevent this.

Your skin helps to rid the body of waste or poisonous matter which it does not want. It also helps to control the amount of heat and water the body loses. And it does these things through the sweat glands. When the body becomes overheated, the sweat glands pump out water from the bloodstream on to the surface of the skin. It does this through special openings called 'pores'. On the skin the water turns into vapour and in so doing draws heat from the body. When the body gets really hot — perhaps on a very hot day, or during lively games — more water is pumped out than can evaporate at once, and then you say a person is sweating. When the body is cold and wants to keep its heat, the pores close up. Even on a cold day, however, some sweating is done, because waste matter from the body is passed out through the pores mixed with the water. Though the skin is constantly allowing water out, it never lets any in. If it did this we should become waterlogged in the bath!

How fast does light travel?

Light travels so fast — 186,281 miles a *second* — that over short distances its speed is hard to imagine. When we press an electric light switch, the light seems to come on that very instant. And so, to all intents and purposes, it does. But it has taken time, however little, to travel from the light bulb to our eye. If light could follow the curve of the earth, it would go round seven times in one second. (It cannot do this, because light travels in straight lines.) Light from the sun takes about eight minutes to reach us on earth — but in that eight minutes it has travelled ninety-three million miles.

7TH FEBRUARY

Whose national flag is an eagle and a snake?

At the end of the twelfth century, the Aztecs invaded Mexico from what we now call California. The land was already occupied by several other civilised peoples, and for many years the Aztecs could not settle there.

Then, legend has it, at a time when they were driven to an unhealthy, marshy area, the Aztec chief, Tenoch, saw an eagle devouring a snake in a fig-tree, and took this as a sign that he should build a city here. So a city was built on piles in the middle of a lake, joined to the mainland by long dykes, which could easily be defended. It was called *Tenochtitlan*, after the chief, or *Mexico* after the Aztec god, Mexitli. It was where Mexico City stands today.

Mexico has gone through many changes of fortune since the days of Tenoch, but the eagle devouring a snake still appears on the country's flag.

What is the difference between a tortoise and a turtle?

What are crustaceans?

The turtle and the tortoise belong to the same family of reptiles, and at first glance they look alike. But their separate ways of life have given them several points of difference. The turtle lives in the sea, only coming ashore to lay eggs, and is a flesh-eater. Tortoises (with the exception of the terrapin, or water tortoise) live on dry land and feed mainly on plants.

The tortoise has stumpy feet and quite a high, oval-shaped shell. Life in the sea has flattened the turtle's shell, made it heartshaped rather than oval, and flattened its feet into paddles. It is unable to draw its head right back into the shell as the tortoise can.

Crustaceans range in size from tiny water-fleas, only just visible to the naked eye, through shrimps, prawns and crayfish, to crabs and lobsters. They are a class of animals without backbones, which have instead a jointed shell covering their bodies. Most of the crustaceans live in either fresh or salt water, but some live on land. The woodlouse, for instance, which can roll its jointed, armoured body into a ball at the approach of danger, is a crustacean.

28

What is fog?

Fog is a mass of small drops of water, sometimes mixed with smoke or dust, which is so dense that it is difficult or impossible to see through it. It is caused by a cooling of the air which turns the water vapour into water drops. Fog at sea is caused by warm air being cooled by the colder water. Smog is a nasty kind of fog which contains a great deal of smoke. It forms over big towns where there are many homes and factory chimneys.

Why is Fort Knox so famous?

If you can imagine all the spare gold of the richest country in the world being collected together and put into one big building, then you will understand why Fort Knox is so famous. It is the chief safe deposit for gold bullion in the United States of America and holds ten thousand *million* dollars' worth of gold bricks. It is, of course, a very strong building. Built in 1936 of granite, steel and concrete, it is bomb-proof and thief-proof. Inside are guards, outside are sentries. The whole building is surrounded by a steel fence and there are lots of 'magic eyes' which sound the alarm if anybody crosses their beams. As if that were not enough, the building stands in the middle of a huge American army camp, which has guards on duty every minute of the day and night.

What is a plateau?

A plateau is a plain, or piece of flat land, standing above the land around it. Plateaux (the word comes from the French, so for more than one we add an 'x' and not an 's') can be fairly small, like the mile-long Table Mountain behind Cape Town, South Africa, or can spread over whole countries, like the vast plateaux of Central Asia which rise in gigantic steps until they reach their highest in the plateau of Tibet.

13TH FEBRUARY

What is a passport?

A passport is a licence, given by the government, to travel abroad. It is also a form of safe-conduct: in the government's name, it asks people in other countries to give you safe passage through their lands. Though a passport entitles you to leave this country, it does not necessarily entitle you to enter another. Some foreign countries insist that you have a *visa* — a licence to enter — before they allow you in. If you want to travel to one of these countries, you can get a visa from its offices in Britain.

14TH FEBRUARY

What custom is observed on St Valentine's Day?

February 14th is the feast of two Christian martyrs named Valentine, but neither has anything to do with the custom, observed by people in many countries, of sending cards, flowers or presents to one's sweetheart on this day. In Britain, the custom is to send a valentine card without signing one's name.

Some people think that the origin of the day as a lovers' festival springs from the legend that birds choose their mates on

February 14th. The real origin of the custom, though, seems to be an the ancient Roman festival in honour of the god Pan. Young people at the festival drew lots for partners, and then exchanged presents. In A.D. 496, Pope Gelasius tried to change the old pagan festival into a Christian one by moving the date of the Lupercalia from February 15th to the Feast of St Valentine on the 14th.

15TH FEBRUARY

Where does paper come from?

Most paper nowadays is made from wood, but it can be made also from straw, flax, or old rags. To make paper from wood, the tree is stripped of its bark, torn to shreds by machinery, then mixed with water and chemicals to form a pulp, or paste. The pulp

is rolled out flat and dried. This process of pulping, rolling and drying is used when paper is made from the other materials we mentioned. Most of the wood comes from forests in Canada, Scandinavia and Russia.

Paper was an Eastern invention which was brought by the Moors to Spain and by returning Crusaders to the rest of Europe. The ancient Egyptians used to write on papyrus. This was a long-lasting paper made by soaking strips of papyrus reed — a kind of bullrush — laying them crosswise to each other, pressing them together, then finally drying and polishing the 'mat' so formed.

How does a snake move?

The greatest surprise to anyone who comes across a snake in the wilds — after the first shock of seeing it — is the speed with which it makes off. It seems strange that an animal with no legs should be able to move so quickly. A snake really 'swims' on dry land. It gets along by rippling, or undulating, the whole length of its body, pushing itself along by a side-to-side wavy movement. When it wants to move slowly — when it is creeping nearer and nearer towards its prey, for instance — it pushes itself along by movements of the large scales on its underside.

Why is Westmister Abbey so famous?

There are many reasons why Westminster Abbey is so well known the world over. It has a long and colourful history and bears reminders of more than thirteen hundred years of England's struggles, glories and disasters.

Its full name is the Collegiate Church of St Peter in Westminster. Legend has it that in the seventh century, St Peter appeared to a fisherman and asked to be taken over the River Thames to a new church which had been built on Thorney Island, a desolate island of twelve hectares in the marshes. The fisherman did St Peter's bidding and was rewarded with a huge catch of salmon.

In 1050, Edward the Confessor, the saintly Saxon king, began the building of a fine new church to replace the old one. It was consecrated on 28th December, 1065, and from this date the Abbey marks its known history. A few days after the consecration, Edward died and was buried within the walls of his Abbey Church.

This church lasted until 1245, when Henry III began to build a new one. The rebuilding which Henry started took more than two hundred and fifty years to complete.

Every English monarch since William the Conqueror, with the exceptions of Edward V and Edward VIII, has been crowned in the Abbey. Even when Oliver Cromwell was made Lord Protector, the ceremony took place there.

A number of English sovereigns besides Edward the Confessor are buried in the Abbey, among them Henry III, Edward I, Edward III, Richard II and Anne of Bohemia, Henry V, Henry VII, Queen Elizabeth I, James I, Charles II, William and Mary, and Queen Anne. The last to be buried there were George II and Queen Caroline.

Also buried there are many famous commoners, among them the explorer and missionary David Livingstone; the statesmen Bonar Law and Neville Chamberlain; the scientists Newton, Darwin and Lister; the musicians Purcell, Gibbons and Stanford. In the South Transept Aisle, known as Poets' Corner, are the graves of Chaucer,

Spenser, Dr Johnson, Sheridan, Browning, Tennyson, Dickens, Hardy, Kipling, and the actors Garrick and Irving. Ben Jonson is buried in the nave.

There are many memorials to other famous people who are buried elsewhere, including one to Sir Winston Churchill. The pilots who died in the Battle of Britain in 1940 have a stained glass window to their memory. The dead of two world wars are represented by the Unknown Warrior, who lies in his tomb near the Great West Door.

Organised occasions of Church and State are not the only exciting events the Abbey has seen. Many other unexpected and sometimes terrible things have happened. At the crowning of William the Conqueror, the Norman guards outside heard shouts from within the church. Thinking their king was in danger, they set fire to the Saxon houses round about. In the twelfth century a quarrel between the Archbishops of Canterbury and York resulted in York being dragged away and beaten. At the coronation of Richard the Lionheart, a bat — thought to be a creature of ill-omen — fluttered around the king as he sat on the throne. Early in the fourteenth century some of the

monks stole treasure from the Chapter House. And in 1378 the murder of a knight during High Mass led to the church being closed for four months.

The Gate House was once used as a prison. There, Sir Walter Raleigh spent the night before his execution. And in the Chapter House, William Caxton set up the first printing press in England.

The Abbey has its own school, Westminster School. Seven prime ministers and ten archbishops have been among the famous old boys.

There are many fine things to see inside the Abbey, including the Coronation Chair which holds the Stone of Scone, the beautiful tracery roof of the Henry VII Chapel, and the magnificent walls and windows of the main church.

But the Abbey is not just a collection of stone and wood, of tombs and memorials. It has been described as 'the parish church of the English-speaking peoples.' As such, and through its beautiful and moving services, it brings joy and comfort to people from all parts of the world. It is a great part of England's past, and of her present and future, too.

Who invented the telephone?

The telephone as we know it was the invention of Alexander Graham Bell (1847—1922) a Scottish scientist who had gone to live in America. Bell's special interest in life was in teaching the deaf, an interest he got from his father, who taught deaf-mutes to speak. His scientific training led him to investigate ways in which human speech could be sent by wire.

In 1870 his father took the family to Canada. Alexander's two brothers had died of tuberculosis, Alexander himself had the disease, and his father thought, rightly, that the Canadian climate would cure it.

In 1871 Alexander's father was asked to train teachers of the deaf in Boston, USA. He could not go, but Alexander went in his stead. In 1873 Alexander became a professor at Boston University. There he experimented, with the help of a man named Thomas Watson, with electrical transmission of telegraph messages. From these experiments he moved on to trying to transmit human speech. A German named J. P. Reis had paved the way by inventing, in 1861, a machine called the *telephone* which could transmit noise and music, but not the human voice.

Bell spent many long hours experimenting with a metal diaphragm placed close to a coil wound round a magnet. On March 10th, 1876, he spilled some acid on his clothes and cried out: 'Mr Watson, come here. I want you.' Watson, in another room, heard the voice over the telephone receiver and rushed to Bell's aid. The first telephone call had been made.

Bell's interest in the deaf lasted all his life, and he used the money from his invention for their benefit. In 1877 he married Mabel Hubbard, one of his students, herself deaf from the age of four.

How does a water tap work?

The part of the tap which you turn is the top end of a screw which goes down into the casing of the tap. At the bottom end of this screw is a rubber or leather washer which presses down on to the end of the water pipe, preventing the water from coming any further. When you turn the tap on, the screw rises, lifting the washer with it and allowing the water to gush up from the pipe and run out through the spout. When you turn off the tap, you are screwing the washer down again on to the pipe and cutting off the flow of water.

19TH FEBRUARY

Are bats blind?

Though a bat is not really blind, its eyes are very weak. We know that a bat can tell light from darkness, but we do not know whether it can actually *see* anything.

For finding its way about, and for chasing the insects on which it feeds, it has a natural radar device which can 'see' objects in the dark.

A bat sends out high-pitched squeaks — so high that humans cannot hear them — and can tell, from the way the echoes return, how far away and what shape an object is. It sends out these sounds through its nostrils, so that even the carrying of a large insect in its mouth does not stop them being given out. Because it does its hunting at night, this method of 'seeing' is of far more use to it than even perfect eyesight would be.

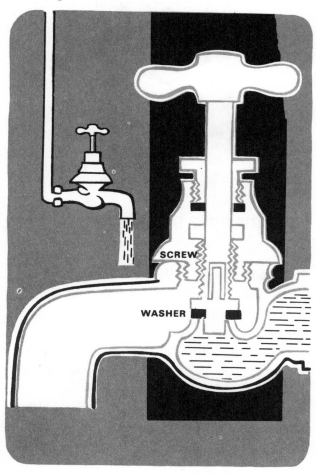

SCREW

WASHER

gas. These gases were dangerous because they caught fire easily, so after a while the gas helium, which was much less inflammable, was used instead.

Balloonists carry bags of sand in the basket so that when the balloon reaches the thin upper air and will rise no further, they can throw some of the sand overboard and make the craft lighter, thus allowing it to rise again. When they want to come down, they let some of the gas out of the bag so that it can no longer lift the weight of the basket and starts to fall gently back to earth.

22ND FEBRUARY

Who was the first President of the United States?

Until the American War of Independence, in 1775, the thirteen states of America were ruled by the British king, who was then George III, and the British parliament at Westminster. The Americans fought against this and set up a republic. The head of their republic, the president, was George Washington.

Washington was born in Virginia in 1732, and established a name for himself as a soldier in wars against the French. He was well enough known in 1775 to be chosen to lead all the American forces. In the beginning, Washington did not want a complete breach with Britain, but when he realised this was the only answer to America's problems, he fought determinedly for independence. It took him some years to discipline his men to beat the British Army, but he did it, mainly through his personal courage and belief in his cause.

21ST FEBRUARY

What makes a balloon rise?

A balloon rises for the same reason that a thing floats on water: because it is lighter than the substance around it, in this case, the air.

Early balloons were lifted by having a fire lit under the bag. The bag, open at the bottom end, was filled with hot air, which is lighter than cold air, and so rose off the ground. Later, balloons were filled with a gas lighter than air, such as hydrogen or coal

After the war, he retired briefly to his estates, but he was the obvious man to become president. He held that office for only two terms, a custom which has been followed ever since, except in war, and retired again to his beloved farm. He died in 1799, and the capital city of the country he helped so much to create was named in his memory.

What is semaphore?

Semaphore is a code in which different positions of the outstretched human arms stand for different letters of the alphabet. It was invented in 1794 by a Frenchman named Chappe, and was widely used for the sending of long-distance messages before the invention of the electric telegraph. An instrument with two mechanical arms — like a double-sided railway signal — was also used to send the messages. This instrument, called a semaphore after the code, is still used today at sea. When the messages are sent by human arms, the sender usually holds a flag in each hand so that the positions may more easily be seen.

24TH FEBRUARY

What is Notre Dame?

Notre Dame (it is French for 'Our Lady', meaning the Virgin Mary, Mother of Christ) is the great cathedral in Paris. Its foundation stones were laid in 1163 on the site of a Christian altar which had earlier been a heathen shrine, on the Ile de la Cité, an island in the River Seine.

Notre Dame is noted for the great beauty of its building, which took about a hundred and fifty years to finish. Its walls, which are lavishly decorated, are supported by beautiful flying buttresses.

Henry VI of England was crowned King of France in Notre Dame in 1431, and Mary Queen of Scots was married there to the Dauphin, the Crown Prince of France.

The French novelist Victor Hugo used it for the setting of his novel *Notre Dame de Paris* (1831), better known as *The Hunchback of Notre Dame*. The novel was eventually made into a film, with Charles Laughton as Quasimodo, the deaf, half-blind hunchback who lived in the cathedral.

Which ancient god had wings on his shoes?

Hermes — the Romans later called him Mercury — was the Greek god of trade, wealth and robbers. He was also the messenger for the other gods on Mount Olympus. To speed him on his errands he wore winged sandals. He also wore a wide-brimmed hat and carried a staff entwined with serpents. He seems to have been a very busy and mischievous god: on the very day he was born he invented the musical instrument called the lyre and then stole fifty cows from the great god Apollo. He drove them backwards so it would appear, from their hoofmarks, that they had been taken in the opposite direction. Despite this, the furious Apollo caught up with him, only to have his anger softened by the gift of the lyre. Hermes then went back to sleep!

What is a swordfish?

There is a whole family of fishes which bears the name 'swordfish', and it is easy to see how the different members of this family got their name. The upper jaw grows into a long, bony, sword-like weapon, which can be used with fearful effect — even to the extent of stabbing holes in the planks of wooden boats. The common swordfish, whose Latin name is *Xiphias gladius*, is sometimes found in European waters. The different members of the family range in length from one to over four metres and the swords of the bigger fish are often as much as a metre long. The swordfish is a relative of the mackerel and, like its cousin, feeds on other fish. It is a favourite quarry of big-game fishermen.

A fish which could be confused with it, at first glance, is the sawfish. However, as the name suggests, the long upper jaw of the saw fish has teeth embedded on either side so that it looks like a double-edged saw. This creature is no relation of the swordfish — it belongs to the shark family.

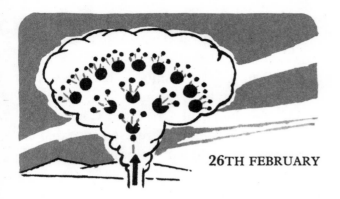

26TH FEBRUARY

Why is uranium so important?

Uranium is a soft, grey metal. Its chief use is to produce atomic power, which is used more and more nowadays to make electricity.

If the use of atomic power is to continue to develop, more uranium must be found. As more countries learn to use atomic power, so the demand for uranium will grow. The main areas in which it is found are Canada, South Africa and Russia, and a great search is going on all over the world to discover more of it.

As well as being a source of cheap and plentiful power for working machinery and lighting our towns and cities, uranium is also the explosive part of the atomic and hydrogen bombs. So it is easy to see why so many people want it, for good and ill.

Who was Abraham?

Abraham was the father, or founder, of the Jewish nation and his story is told in Genesis, the first book of the Bible.

Abraham and his family — his father, his wife Sarah and his nephew Lot, travelled from their home in Ur of the Chaldees to a place called Haran. There, God appeared to Abraham and told him to go into the Land of Canaan.

So Abraham, Sarah, Lot, and their servants and animals set off for Canaan. There came a time when there was not enough water for all the beasts. So Abraham told Lot to choose which way he would go. Whichever it was, Abraham would take the opposite path.

Lot chose the fertile plain of Jordan, leaving Abraham in the stony mountains. God spoke again to Abraham and told him that He would give to him and his descendants for ever all the land he could see around him.

When Abraham reached the age of ninety-nine, and still had no children, God told him that his wife, Sarah, would bear a son who would be called Isaac. The son was born and grew into a fine boy, dearly loved by old Abraham and his wife.

One day God told Abraham to take the boy into the mountains and there kill him as a sacrifice. Abraham took his son, bound him and was about to use the knife, when God told him to hold his hand. Abraham had proved, said the Lord, that he loved Him enough to sacrifice his only son. Abraham lifted up his eyes and saw a ram in a thicket: this he sacrificed instead.

After all his difficulties, Abraham died at a very great age. He had shown himself to be a worthy father of God's chosen race, and it was from him, through Isaac, that the Jewish people of the Old Testament were descended.

What is the meaning of March?

It is probably fitting that March, with its wild winds and sudden squalls of rain, should be named after a god of war. Mars was the Roman god of war, always shown as a fierce, bearded figure clad in armour and helmet and carrying a spear and a shield. He was more than a war god: he was also the god of farming, and prayers were said to him when fields were made ready for sowing. March is the month of Mars because it marks the beginning of the season when war and farming, two of the most important activities in a Roman's life, could start again.

What does 'Gothic' mean?

'Gothic' is a term used to describe the style of architecture and arts flourishing in Western Europe before the Renaissance, and revived in the nineteenth century.

A typical and beautiful building in the Gothic style, with pointed arches, high walls, stained-glass windows, soaring slender pillars and delicate stone tracery, is Cologne Cathedral. Notre Dame in Paris is another.

Can water run uphill?

If you were to let go of this book, it would fall to the ground, pulled there by the force of gravity which holds everything down to the surface of the earth. When you picked up the book it would still be the same shape because it is a solid object, able to keep its shape unless force is applied to change it.

If, however, you emptied a glass of water on to the ground, the water would spread out and drain away, by running down a slope or into cracks in the ground. This is because water is liquid, has no shape of its own, and is drawn by the pull of gravity to the lowest point it can reach. The reason that rivers run to the sea is that the level of the sea is lower than that of the surrounding land.

So water, in its free state, cannot run uphill. Engineers, however, can send water across a valley simply by laying a pipe down the side of one hill and up the side of another. The water runs through the pipe, first down the hill and then up the other side, and it would appear to be running uphill. It is, however, not really running — it is being pushed by the weight of the water in the pipe behind it.

Since the water cannot get out of the enclosed pipe, it goes on being pushed upwards until it reaches the level of the water on the other side of the valley. It cannot be pushed higher than this, because gravity pulls equally on a body of water to make it level over all its surface.

4TH MARCH

Can fish hear?

You have probably read, and will read many more times, about the 'silent' world of the fishes. Nothing could be further from the truth: the underwater world is as noisy as dry land to those creatures fitted by nature for life there.

Fish are very well equipped for hearing. They have, to start with, a pair of ears. These ears have not outside parts as ours have, but are simply tiny holes on either side of the head, leading to the inner ear. Because there is no outside structure to direct the

sound, these ears are probably not as good as our own, but the fish has more ways than this of picking up sounds, or vibrations in the water.

Along each side of the fish's body is a line of little holes, or pores, which can also pick up vibrations and changes of pressure in the water — perhaps denoting the approach of an enemy — and pass on the message to the brain. This line of pores is called the lateral line, and can be seen quite easily.

Lastly, fish of the carp family — this includes our familiar goldfish — have tiny bones in the head which are linked with the swim bladder. The swim bladder, a taut, air-filled 'balloon' which keeps the fish upright in the water — also acts as a sounding board which can pick up and magnify the tiniest vibrations, and pass these along the bones directly to the inner ear.

For all these reasons you must move very quietly along the bank when you go fishing. You cannot hear the fish — but they can certainly hear you.

What is Shrove Tuesday?

Shrove Tuesday is the last day before Lent, the long period of Christian fasting. It was the day when people went to the priest to be *shriven* — to confess their sins and be granted pardon — and from this it gets its name.

Because it was the last day before the fast, it was a day of great feasting and merrymaking. It was also the day when people finished up all the rich food in their store-cupboards. That is how we got the custom of eating pancakes on Shrove Tuesday.

What is Ash Wednesday?

Ash Wednesday is the first day of Lent, the Christian fast of forty days which comes before Easter. Its name comes from the old custom of putting ashes on the head as a sign of penitence.

What is the Kremlin?

'Kremlin' comes from a Russian word meaning 'citadel' or 'fortress'.

When we use the word 'Kremlin' however, we mean the old centre of Moscow, whose buildings have survived fire and destruction in various wars over the centuries. The Moscow Kremlin stands on a hill and is surrounded by a great wall, one and a half miles long and twenty metres high. Among its buildings are those which house the Supreme Soviet of the U.S.S.R., the government of Russia. It also contains some splendid palaces which were once the homes of the Czars, but which are now museums, and two beautiful golden-domed cathedrals.

8TH MARCH

What is migration?

Migration is a movement of herds or flocks of animals to places where they will find more food and water, have better weather, or will be able to have their young and rear them in suitable surroundings.

Every year, herds of animals in Africa, such as the wildebeeste, zebra and antelope, travel vast distances, eating the grass of the plains as they go, and return by the same routes. The buffalo used to do the same thing in North America before the great herds were wiped out. In the north of Canada, caribou and reindeer move south in the winter to escape the worst of the snow and ice.

There are great yearly movements of birds, too. In the autumn many of our birds fly away to warmer lands, some of them flying more than four thousand miles. At the same time, from colder parts of the world, such as the Arctic regions, birds fly into Europe to spend the winter.

Another kind of migration is that of the salmon and the eel. The salmon, hatched in a stream in Scotland, will make its way to the open sea and live there for several years. When it becomes adult, it will swim back to the very stream where it was born to lay its eggs. Eels are hatched in the Sargasso Sea, a strange seaweed-tangled stretch of water off the American coast. From there they migrate to the coasts their parents came from, and swim up rivers to live in fresh water for from five to fifteen years. Then they return across the Atlantic to the Sargasso Sea to lay their eggs, and when this is done they die. Nobody knows why the salmon and the eel undertake such long and dangerous journeys to lay their eggs in a particular place when many others, it seems, would do just as well.

45

9TH MARCH

What is the 24-hour clock?

We are used to telling the time by dividing each day of twenty-four hours into two periods of twelve hours. Your clock at home is numbered from one to twelve and, of course, when you look at the time you know whether it is ten o'clock in the morning or ten o'clock at night. But this way of telling the time can become confusing if people are arranging to meet each other or catch a train or boat or aeroplane. The difficulty can be overcome by adding 'in the morning' or 'in the evening' to the time stated, or by adding 'A.M.' or 'P.M.' which are short for the Latin words meaning 'before noon' and 'after noon'. Though this is generally enough for ordinary people making arrangements with each other, it is still confusing and likely to give rise to misunderstandings, in a complicated timetable.

To avoid such mistakes, many institutions have for a long time been using the twenty-four hour method to tell the time. This numbers the hours of the day right through from One to Twenty-four. A min-

ute past midnight, then, becomes 00.01 hours (no hours, one minute); 12 noon is 12.00 hours (called twelve hundred hours because of the two noughts which show there are no minutes involved). One o'clock in the afternoon becomes 13.00 hours, two o'clock becomes 14.00 hours and so on. Minutes are given as minutes *after* the hour, not *to* the hour, so that quarter to three in the afternoon becomes 14.45. The complete table is as follows:

01.00 — 1 a.m.	13.00 — 1 p.m.
02.00 — 2 a.m.	14.00 — 2 p.m.
03.00 — 3 a.m.	15.00 — 3 p.m.
04.00 — 4 a.m.	16.00 — 4 p.m.
05.00 — 5 a.m.	17.00 — 5 p.m.
06.00 — 6 a.m.	18.00 — 6 p.m.
07.00 — 7 a.m.	19.00 — 7 p.m.
08.00 — 8 a.m.	20.00 — 8 p.m.
09.00 — 9 a.m.	21.00 — 9 p.m.
10.00 — 10 a.m.	22.00 — 10 p.m.
11.00 — 11 a.m.	23.00 — 11 p.m.
12.00 — 12 a.m.	24.00 — 12 p.m.

10TH MARCH

Why do we need sleep?

When a motor car has been running for a certain length of time, it has to go into a garage for an overhaul. It is cleaned and mended and any little faults put right so that they do not become any worse. Finally, it is filled up with petrol, the batteries are re-charged, and fresh water is put in the radiator.

This is what happens to our bodies and minds when we go to sleep. With all activity stopped, the body has a chance to do some repair work. Poisons and waste are cleared from the bloodstream, damaged cells are

replaced, tense muscles are relaxed, rested, and re-fuelled for the next day, so that we wake up feeling lively and refreshed and not tired as we did when we went to bed. Even some of our dreams are part of this clearing-out process. Many of the things we have been worrying about during the day are dealt with by our brain at night. During the working-out of these problems, we receive impressions of them — often in highly disguised forms — in the shape of dreams.

Children need much more sleep than adults, firstly because they use up a great deal of energy in their play, and secondly because their bodies have to provide new cells for growth as well as replace the old ones.

What was the Renaissance?

The Renaissance was a period in the fifteenth and sixteenth centuries in which the learning and arts of Europe suddenly blossomed forth with great vigour and paved the way for the old world of the Middle Ages to develop into the one we know today.

European society in the Middle Ages was feudal: people were divided into nobles, peasants who worked for them, and church-men. Most people lived in the country, and were either soldiers or worked on the land. Towns were few and very small. Few people could read, and learning and the arts were left almost entirely to monks and priests.

With the discovery of new trade routes on the seas, and new countries, like America, a new class sprang up of merchants and businessmen. Towns, which were mainly trading centres, became larger, and the people who lived in them were neither soldiers nor farmers, but wealthy and intelligent people, eager for new ideas. Poetry, painting, sculpture, music and architecture all reflected their imagination and experience of life, which were wider than those of mediaeval men.

Instead of being specialists in one thing, people sought to have knowledge of everything, to become 'complete men'. Leonardo da Vinci, for example, was not only a great painter, but also a sculptor, a musician, a biologist, an engineer, and an architect.

The word 'renaissance' means 'rebirth'. 'Being born again' describes very well what did happen to the development of human activity.

What is another name for a river horse?

The Greek words for 'horse' and 'river' are *hippos* and *potamus*. You can guess from this that the river horse is our fat old friend, the hippopotamus. He was named the river horse by Pliny the Elder, the Roman writer, and, indeed, when only part of his head and neck are showing above the water, he does look like a horse. He is, however, a pig, a distant relation of our farmyard porker. The second largest land animal (the largest is the elephant), an adult hippo weighs three or four tonnes and measures up to four and a half metres long. He feeds only on plants, but feeds very well — on one hundred and eighty kilograms of food at a time.

Could people live on the moon?

Now that man has landed on the moon the next stage will be to make the place ready to receive more visitors.

From what we know about the moon, life will not be very pleasant there. The surface is covered with great craters and high jagged mountains. There are also great 'seas' of solidified lava — rock which was once molten but has now cooled and hardened. The seas and the hollows of the craters are covered with a layer of volcanic dust. There is no air, no water, no animals or plants. Nor is there any sound, because sound needs air to carry it. During the day, which lasts for a fortnight, the rocks become hotter than boiling water. During the night, which also lasts for a fortnight, the temperature drops to 83 degrees Centigrade below freezing.

So the people who go to the moon will not be able to go out for a walk unless they wear a space suit to protect them from the heat or cold and to supply them with air to breathe. Houses on the moon will have to be completely sealed in, like a diving bell, and everything people need, even air itself, will have to be brought from earth.

What are the Ides of March?

The Ides were one of the three fixed days in each month of the Roman calendar system. The other fixed days were the *calends* and the *nones*. The peculiar thing about them is that the Romans counted backwards from them. The first day of each month was the *calends*. The *nones* were on the ninth day before the *ides,* on the 5th or 7th day, depending on which month it happened to be. The *ides* were the 15th day of March, May, July and October, and the 13th day of the other months. Compared to our own calendar, this seems a very involved way of working out the date!

The Ides of March are famous because in the play *Julius Caesar* by William Shakespeare, Caesar was warned by a soothsayer to 'beware the Ides of March'. He meant that Caesar should watch out for danger on the 15th of March. And it was on that day that Caesar was murdered.

14TH MARCH

What is strange about the Tower of Pisa?

At Pisa, a town in Italy, a great cathedral was begun in the year 1063. One of the most splendid parts of the cathedral was to be the campanile, or bell tower, which was built in the year 1173. The cathedral has indeed been famous for this bell tower because the tower *leans*. It was not meant to do this, but the ground around Pisa is soft and marshy, and the man who built the tower did not put in firm enough foundations. The top of the tower is now over four and a half metres out of true, and every year it leans a little farther over. In time, if this movement is not halted, the tower will fall to the ground. The Italian government is holding a competition for designs which will stop any further leaning. Meanwhile, Pisa is famous for its Leaning Tower.

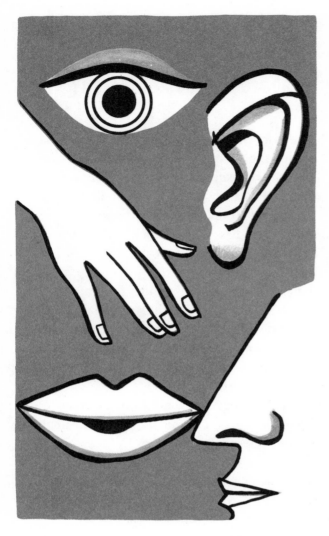

'wits'. Scientists are investigating a sixth sense, which they call extra-sensory perception. This is something which many people have, but about which very little is known. For instance, when two friends, separated perhaps by miles, think of the same thing at the same time, it would appear that thought-messages have been sent from one to the other. Certain people are mind-readers and can pick up the thoughts of someone else, even though that person has not said a word.

17TH MARCH

Who is the patron saint of Ireland?

16TH MARCH

What are our senses?

Sight, hearing, touch, taste and smell are the senses through which we receive our impressions of the world around us. Through these senses our brain knows just where we are, what we are doing, how we are feeling, and what is going on about us. Without them — try and imagine yourself having none of these things — we should just be a collection of vegetables. These senses together are known as the Five Senses or

The patron saint of Ireland is St Patrick. He was born, probably near Dumbarton in Scotland, about the year 387. He became a monk in France and was given the task by the Pope of converting Ireland to Christianity. Legend has it that he explained the mystery of the Trinity, that God is one God yet three persons, by showing the Irish a shamrock, which is like a clover, one leaf but three parts. The shamrock is now the emblem of Ireland.

March 17th is the anniversary of his death — though it is not certain in what year he died — and this is celebrated as St Patrick's Day.

4b

Why are birds' eggs of different colours?

Eggs in a nest have to be left from time to time while the mother bird goes in search of food. And there are many creatures — including other birds, snakes, squirrels, rats, and men — who like nothing better to eat than a nice fresh egg. Nature has given birds a way of foiling these enemies: the eggs are coloured, speckled, or streaked with wiggly lines to make them blend with the material of the nest, and so become hard to see from anything but very close range.

The snipe lays her eggs in a hollow among coarse meadow grasses, and the eggs are spotted and blotched with large markings which look just like the rough grass around them. The little tern lays her eggs among the pebbles of the beach, and the speckled colouring and shape of the eggs make them look just like pebbles. There are many examples of this protective colouring.

Birds which have no need to disguise their eggs — those which make their nest in a hollow tree, or in holes or burrows, or build a home which is covered from all sides — generally lay white or light-coloured eggs which would be easily spotted if they were laid out in the open.

Perhaps the strangest example of protective colouring is that of the cuckoo's eggs. The mother cuckoo lays her egg in the nest of another bird, taking out one of the eggs already there and replacing it with one of her own. The egg that she lays is almost the same in colouring and markings to those in the nest! A collection of cuckoo's eggs from different nests looks like a collection from different birds.

What is a pygmy?

Pygmies are a race of unusually short human beings who live in parts of Africa and Asia. The African pygmies (Negrillos) live in the Ituri Forest of the Congo basin, and in Burundi, Cameroon, Gabon and Rwanda. They generally measure between 1.34 metres and 1.42 metres tall. A pygmy man who reached the height of 1.49 metres would consider himself very tall indeed. They are a shy, simple people and live deep in the forest. They keep no animals, sow no crops, wear little clothing, and build only the flimsiest of shelters to sleep in. They live by hunting and trapping animals, fishing, and gathering fruit, roots, nuts and honey. They hunt mainly with the bow and poisoned arrows, though some tribes also make use of spears.

Pygmies live in small groups, led by the oldest man. Though they generally keep to the forest, they emerge occasionally to trade meat and fruit with negro tribes for salt and iron tools and weapons.

Asian pygmies (Negritos) live in Malaya, Sumatra, New Guinea, the Andaman Islands and the Philippines. Like their African cousins, they live simple, backward lives in the deep forests.

Why is Samuel Plimsoll remembered?

What was the Domesday Book?

When William the Conqueror was finally in control of all of England, he wanted to know how much tax he could take from each farm and village. He could not tax people without knowing what money and possessions they had, so in 1086 he sent men all over the country to find out. They made lists of all the people and all the land and animals which they owned. These lists were put together in one big book — the Domesday Book. The Domesday Book still exists today, in the Public Record Office in London, and gives us a very good idea of what life in those days was like.

Samuel Plimsoll was a British Member of Parliament in the last century who spent all his life working for better conditions for seamen. He was very concerned about the number of sailors drowned at sea because the ships they sailed in were overloaded and in a bad state of repair.

His efforts resulted in the introduction, in 1876, of the Plimsoll Line. This is a mark on the side of a ship — a circle with a straight line drawn through it — which shows the level in the water to which a ship can be safely loaded. The 'plimsoll' shoes you wear for playing games were also named after him, because they are so useful to seamen and sailors.

Who invented the first motor car?

You can, if you wish, trace the motor car right back to the steam carriage built in 1770 by the Frenchman called Nicholas Cugnot. The car as we know it, however, was the work of two Germans, who did not know each other, named Daimler and Benz. In 1884 Benz produced a vehicle driven by a spirit-fuelled engine. In 1885 Daimler produced a better engine, which was used by a French firm in 1887 to drive vehicles whose basic shape was very much like that of our modern cars.

The petrol-driven car soon took over from the steam carriage. It was smaller, neater, easier to drive — and much safer. In Britain, in 1865, a law had been passed limiting the speed of motor vehicles to four miles an hour, and insisting that a man with a red flag should walk in front of the vehicle. This law, which had been passed partly because of the opposition by railway and stagecoach companies to the steam carriage, but also because people were frightened of the snorting, clanking vehicles, was repealed in 1896. Meanwhile, however, it had discouraged British inventors from working on motor cars.

Motor car design improved rapidly, mainly in France, in the last years of the nineteenth century. Then, in 1901, Ransom E. Olds began to use assembly-line methods to build cars in the United States. The cars moved along the factory on a trolley and workmen assembled them one after the other, each man fitting on a particular part. This made the cars much cheaper to produce. In 1909 Henry T. Ford took up the idea and decided to produce even cheaper cars by making only one model. This was his famous Model T. In 1913 he switched from trolleys to conveyor belts, and this made production still faster and cheaper, paving the way for the multitude of cheap family cars on the roads today.

What is a calendar?

The word 'calendar' comes from the Latin word for account book and it means the division of the year, like a set of accounts, into its days, weeks and months. Most of the world uses the Roman calendar, which gives us 365 days in a year, and 366 days every fourth, or leap, year. The extra day every four years is to make up for the fact that a year — which is the time taken for the earth to go once round the sun — is a few hours longer than 365 days. There are several other calendars besides the Christian one — Jewish and Mohammedan for instance — and from time to time people have produced ideas for new ways of dividing the year. Most of these new ideas, however, proved no better than the old ones.

24TH MARCH

Where does rubber come from?

Rubber is made from the sap of a South American tree. This sap, called latex, is collected by making slanting cuts in the bark of the tree and placing a cup at the bottom to collect the sap as it oozes out. At first rubber was collected from trees growing wild in Brazil, but the coming of the motor car meant that much more was needed for the making of tyres, so young trees were taken from South America to Malaya and Indonesia, and today all three places have vast rubber plantations.

Why does a giraffe have such a long neck?

The giraffe feeds on leaves and twigs of trees which grow on the African plains. Though the lower parts of these trees are stripped by smaller animals, such as the antelopes, there is still plenty of food left for the giraffe. His long neck and legs and his tongue, which is eighteen inches long, mean that he can eat the leaves from the tops of the trees. Though his neck is so long, there are only the same number of bones in it — seven — that there are in other animals. This means it is not very flexible, and to get his head down to drink water, the giraffe has to straddle out his legs in a very inelegant way.

25TH MARCH

Which is the oldest university in Europe?

The early universities grew from the schools set up around mediaeval monasteries and cathedrals. Which was the first is still open to question. As long ago as A.D. 900 there was a medical school at Salerno, Italy, but as it taught only medicine, it does not really count. The honour of being the first belongs either to the University of Bologna, in Italy, or the University of Paris, both of which were in existence before 1200. The subjects studied were philosophy, medicine and law.

What is a microphone?

A microphone is an instrument which turns sound — voices, music and so on — into 'patterns' in an electrical current.

The most common type of microphone has a thin sheet of carbon — a diaphragm — which vibrates when sound waves hit it. Behind this diaphragm is a space, loosely packed with grains of carbon. As the diaphragm vibrates it keeps pressing these grains of carbon, squeezing them together and letting them go again. This squeezing and releasing action alters the pattern of the electric current which is flowing through the grains. The electric current can then be sent over great distances, either through wires or through the air, and turned back into sound by loudspeakers such as we have in our radio sets.

27TH MARCH

What is an earthquake?

Earthquakes are reminders that our globe is changing all the time. The outer crust is slowly cooling and shrinking. Beneath this crust a great mass of molten rock is constantly pressing upwards. This means that the cooling rocks of the earth's crust are always under great stress, being pulled one way or pushed another, and from time to time this stress results in a sudden movement of the ground along a fault, or line of weakness. This sudden movement is an earthquake. At the heart of the disturbance the movement is very violent, shaking down buildings and causing landslides and tidal waves. The shock waves from an earthquake spread out in all directions, getting weaker as they travel, but are often still strong enough to be picked up by sensitive instruments on the other side of the world.

What is water?

Most of your body is made of water. Without it you could not live, nor could any other form of life on earth.

Water is a colourless, tastless liquid, and is made up of hydrogen and oxygen, two gases which are found in the air. There are two parts of hydrogen to one part oxygen, and this gives us the chemical symbol for water: H_2O. In its natural state, as river, pond or sea-water, it contains dissolved minerals and salt.

Like other chemicals, water can exist in three states: as a solid, as a liquid and as a gas. The solid state is ice, and the gas is steam — not the steam you can see, for this is made of water droplets, but the invisible vapour like that nearest the spout of a boiling kettle.

What is a plastic?

Plastics are made from many different substances and in many different ways. Basically, however, a plastic is a material which at some stage in its manufacture has been 'plastic', that is, soft enough to be shaped and moulded. This shaping and moulding is done either by heat, by pressure, or by both.

Plastics are one of three groups of chemical compounds called polymers (the other polymers are elastomers — materials like rubber which can stretch — and fibres, like silk). They can be made from natural polymers like cellulose, which is obtained from trees, or from man-made polymers.

Up to the 1930s practically the only plastics known were celluloid and bakelite. Since then, many new kinds have been developed for all sorts of uses. Among them are nylon, polythene, Terylene, polystyrene and polyvinyl chloride, better known as PVC.

What is a windmill?

A windmill is a device for turning machinery by the power of the wind. Four or more large arms covered by canvas or wooden sails are blown round by the wind and, by a series of shafts and cog-wheels, turn the machinery in the building below. Before the coming of steam and electric power windmills were used for grinding corn. These old-fashioned mills were very beautiful. They were generally built on a hill, or in long stretches of flat, open ground, to catch the wind. Holland, because it is flat and much of it is below sea-level, might easily be flooded, either by the sea or by the big rivers which flow through it, so the water from the rivers is diverted into canals, and there are many windmills, which act as pumps, to keep the water-level under control.

A modern type of windmill is used in dry parts of America and Australia for pumping up water from below the ground. This mill, which is not nearly so beautiful as the old kind, has a circle of many small sails set on the top of a high tower of metal scaffolding.

What is the meaning of April?

There is some doubt about the precise meaning of 'April'. The Romans held the month sacred to Venus, goddess of love, and some people think that 'April' comes from her Greek name of Aphrodite. It seems more likely that the name comes from the Latin word *aperire*, which means *to open*. The thought of April as the opener of the year is a very apt one, for it is in April — after the wind and rain of March — that the year really starts to open, with the weather turning soft and gentle and all the leaf and early blossom unfolding on the trees. The custom of calling April 1st 'All Fools Day' seems to date from old celebrations of the beginning of spring.

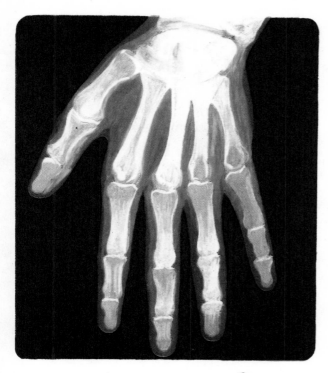

What is an X-ray?

X-rays are invisible rays which can pass through solid objects. They were discovered by a German professor, Wilhelm Röntgen, in 1895, and have since been put to many uses. Doctors use them to take photographs of the inside of our bodies so that they can tell if bones are broken, or if disease is attacking important organs such as our lungs or stomach.

X-rays used without care can be dangerous, because in large doses they are harmful to living tissue. Even this can be turned to good use, however, in the destruction of diseased cells within the body.

Other uses of X-rays are in testing blocks of metal and other materials for flaws, finding out whether paintings and jewellery are genuine, and for discovering more about the way solid matter is formed.

How does a fish swim?

A fish has been wonderfully well fitted by nature for its life in the water. It is streamlined, first of all, so that it slips through the water with the least possible effort. Most of its swimming is done by moving its body from side to side, pushing at the water behind it and so propelling itself forward. For a quick start it will give a flick with its tail. The tail and the fins, though they help the fish in forward movement, are used mainly for changing direction and for steadying the fish in the water. It is perhaps unfair to call them 'extras', but a fish which has lost them can still swim — though not as well as before.

What is Braille?

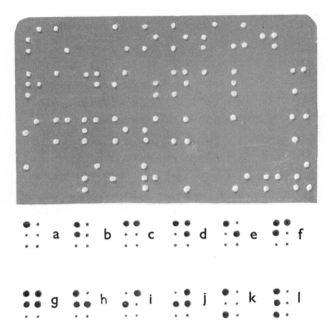

Braille — say 'brale' — is an alphabet by which the blind can read and write. Each letter is made up of raised dots, like the dots on a domino. With the aid of Braille, a blind person can not only read, but can read as fast as someone with sight. There are devices for writing in Braille, a Braille typewriter, and even a Braille shorthand.

The system was invented by a Frenchman called Louis Braille, who lived at the beginning of the last century. He himself was blind as the result of a childhood accident. While he was being educated in Paris he realised that the blind could never make their way in the world if they were not able to read books. He spent several years working out codes, and finally had the idea of basing his alphabet on the six dots of a domino. Braille spread rapidly and is now in use all over the world.

Which is the largest flying bird?

There are three claimants for the title of the largest flying bird. It really depends whether you measure them by wingspan, weight or wing area.

The paauw, or South African bustard, is the *heaviest*. The cock birds have an average weight of forty pounds.

The bird with the *longest wingspan* is the albatross, the mysterious bird which spends its life far out to sea. The longest measured was 3.4 metres, but there are sure to

be others with spans of 3.6 metres.

The bird whose wings cover the most *space*, or area, is the South American vulture called the condor.

Weight, wingspan or wing area? We shall leave the choice to you.

What do muscles do?

Every movement we make is made by our muscles. Whether we are walking, running, jumping, turning cartwheels or just standing up, our muscles are doing things for us by pulling our bones in the way that we want them to go. Muscles are made of many fine fibres about 25 millimetres long. When a muscle gets a message from the brain through a nerve, these fibres become shorter and thicker so that the whole muscle contracts and pulls with it the bone to which it is connected. You see this for yourself by bending your arms and feeling your biceps, the muscle of your upper arm, with the other hand. Do you feel the biceps becoming shorter and thicker? If you clench your teeth you will feel the muscles on either side of your jaw doing the same. Imagine this thing happening all over your body

when you are doing something really active.

Even when we stand still we are using muscles to hold us upright. You can test this by letting yourself go limp.

Some muscles, like those of our tummy, act as a protective covering for our softer parts as well as helping us move.

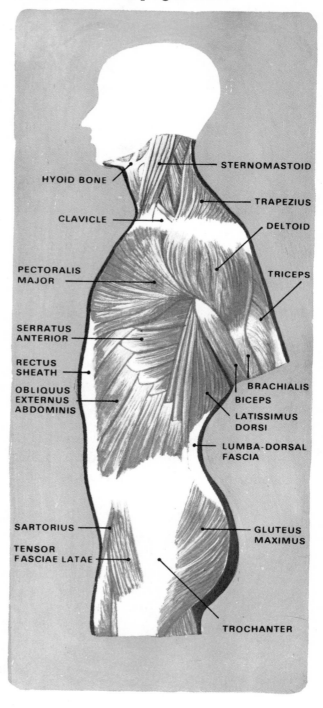

63

after twelve years' absence. Her strange French ways were not popular there, especially since she was a Roman Catholic, while Scotland was in the midst of the Reformation (*20th April*).

She was even more unpopular when, in 1567, she married the man suspected of murdering her second husband, Lord Darnley. She had to flee to England, where, as heir to the throne, she became centre of many Catholic plots against her Protestant cousin, Queen Elizabeth, who kept her prisoner, until, after eighteen years, she was forced to have Mary beheaded.

8TH APRIL

What is the sun?

For us on earth, the sun looms large in the sky, giving us light and heat. Without this giant ball of fire we could not live: our planet would freeze up overnight. Compared with the earth, it is indeed huge. Its width, or diameter, is 864,000 miles, 109 times the diameter of the earth. A million earths could be packed into it.

The sun is the centre of the solar system: a collection of small planets, including our own, which revolve around it. It is a star,

7TH APRIL

Who was Mary Queen of Scots?

Mary Stuart (1542—87) became Queen of Scots when she was one week old. At six, she was sent to France to be educated to marry the King's oldest son.

In 1560, her husband, now Francis II of France, and her mother, who had been ruling Scotland, both died. Mary returned home

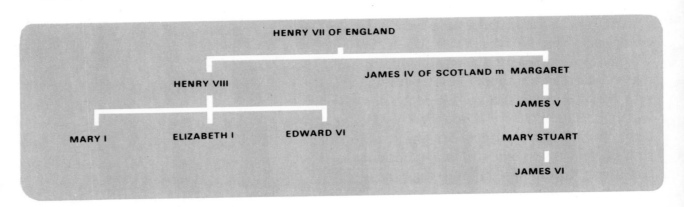

64

but not a very big one: it is just one medium-sized one among all the millions of others in space.

Though it looks solid, the sun is really a mass of intensely hot gas. Even at its very centre it is made of gas. This gas is being burned up all the time, giving off a great amount of heat, because the sun is a gigantic nuclear explosion, very similar to the explosion of a hydrogen bomb. This explosion however, is kept from spreading into space by a layer of gas around the sun's core.

Perhaps the most important thing of all for us is that the sun gives us life itself, and will go on doing so for hundreds of millions of years to come.

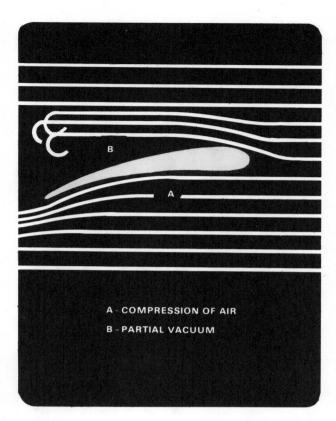

A - COMPRESSION OF AIR
B - PARTIAL VACUUM

9TH APRIL

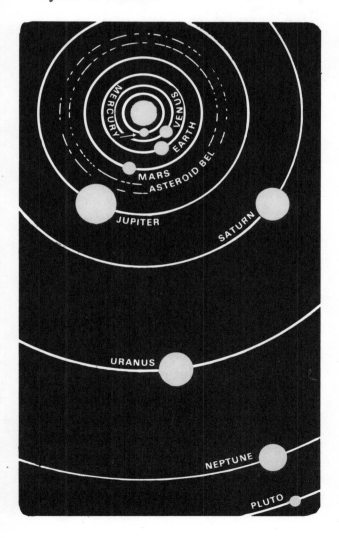

What keeps an aeroplane up in the sky?

You probably know that the front edge of an aeroplane's wing is thick, and that the back edge is thin and that seen from the side, the wing has a downward curve. When the machine is pushed forward by its engines, this shape of the wing compresses, or squeezes, the air below it and thins out the air above it. It is easy to see what happens now: the air below pushes back and lifts the wing. An aeroplane stays up because this process of squeezing the air under the wing is going on all the time. If a plane's engines suddenly stop, it can no longer keep pushing the wings against the air, and the craft falls back to earth.

What is the Salvation Army?

The Salvation Army is a religious body run on army lines, with generals and colonels, corporals and privates. It was begun as a Christian Mission in the East End of London in 1865 by a man named William Booth, and changed its name to the Salvation Army in 1878. The Army has always done much for the poor and needy and runs many hostels and homes both in Britain and abroad. You may have seen a Salvation Army band, in their distinctive uniforms, playing at an open-air service, and have noticed how lively the tunes are. This is because General Booth, tired of dreary hymns, decided to have jaunty music instead, saying 'Why should the devil have all the best tunes?'

11TH APRIL

What is a reptile?

Reptiles are cold-blooded, scaly creatures which breathe air through lungs and lay eggs. They are half-way in the scale of life between amphibians (frogs, newts and toads) and birds. There are five orders, or kinds of living reptiles: the tortoises and turtles; the crocodiles and alligators; the lizards, the snakes; and finally one creature all on its own called the Tuatera.

The giant of the reptile family is the great Anaconda, the South American snake, often nine metres long. One shot by an explorer was nineteen metres long. The most fearsome reptiles are the great crocodiles which live in Africa, Asia and Australia.

In Britain we have six reptiles. Three are

snakes and three are lizards. The grass snake and the smooth snake are harmless, but the adder, or viper, is poisonous. The three lizards are the common lizard, the sand lizard and the slow worm, or blind worm. This last creature is neither slow, nor blind, nor a worm — nor, though he looks like one, is he a snake! He is a lizard whose legs have disappeared through lack of use.

What is radar?

The name 'radar' comes from the words *RA*dio *D*etection *A*nd *R*anging. Radar is a way of seeing things over long distances in darkness or through heavy cloud. It works by sending out radio waves which bounce back from any object they encounter. These returning waves can be picked up and will form in a cathode-ray tube — like the tube of your television set — a 'map' of the countryside or sea round about. On this map will appear any moving objects such as ships or aeroplanes.

Radar was first used during the 1939—45 war, when it played a big part in locating German bombers flying to England in 1940. It has been of great benefit in time of peace: with its help, ships can sail safely and aircraft can land without mishap even in fog.

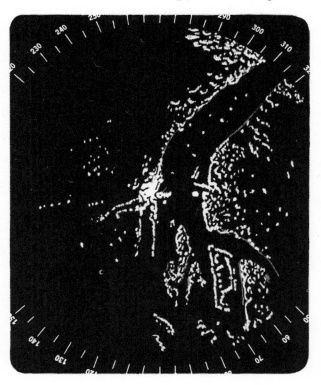

Who first reached the South Pole?

In the year 1911, an exciting and dangerous race over the Antarctic ice was going on between two parties of explorers. At that time nobody had reached the South Pole. A Norwegian expedition under Captain Roald Amundsen and a British expedition under Captain Robert Falcon Scott were each trying to get there before the others. Amundsen reached the Pole first, on December 16th, 1911. He had the advantages over Scott of setting off earlier, of using well-

13TH APRIL

How do humming-birds make their humming noise?

The tiny, dazzling humming-birds take their food from the flowers of the South American jungles, darting from one to the other and hovering to sip nectar with their long tongues or to catch tiny insects. This darting, hovering flight means that the humming-birds' wings must beat very fast, in some cases up to eighty times a second. This fast beating of the tiny wings sets up the humming noise which gives the birds their name. The flight of the humming-bird uses up energy very quickly, and to keep alive he needs fifty to sixty meals a day.

trained dogs instead of ponies, and of not being hampered by having to make scientific observations on the way. Scott's party reached the Pole on January 17th, 1912, and were bitterly disappointed to find that Amundsen had been there a month before them. Tragedy overtook Scott's party on the terrible return journey across 880 miles of polar ice. On the 17th February one of their number, Petty Officer Evans, died. A month later another, Captain Oates, who was suffering badly from frostbite, walked out into the snow to die so that he would not hold the others back. The remaining three — Scott, Dr Wilson and Lieutenant Bowers were caught in a blizzard just eleven miles from their food depot, and died of starvation.

Which is the largest living animal?

Think of the largest African elephant you have seen in the zoo. Now imagine an animal as long as ten elephants and as heavy as twenty, and there you have the largest living animal — the Rorqual, or Blue Whale. Over thirty metres long, more than a hundred and twenty tonnes in weight, the Blue Whale dwarfs even the montrous dinosaurs that once roamed the earth. And yet this huge creature feeds mainly on tiny shrimps.

Who was Yuri Gagarin?

Yuri Alekseyevich Gagarin, a Russian Air Force pilot, was the first man ever to make a flight in space. On April 12th, 1961, at the controls of the space-ship Vostok, he flew right around the earth in one hour and forty-eight minutes. He flew at a height of a hundred and eighty-seven miles and at a top speed of eighteen thousand miles an hour. He was killed in an air crash in 1968.

17TH APRIL

What is a buoy?

A buoy is a large float of wood or metal, moored in rivers or in the sea to mark channels, rocks and sandbanks. Often a buoy will carry a bell or a light on top to make it easier to find. Buoys used around the coast of Britain have different shapes and colours to tell the ships on which side they should pass.

18TH APRIL

Who was Pan?

Pan seems to have been one of the jolliest of the old Greek gods. The son of Hermes, or Mercury, he was a god of the country-side and of flocks and herds. He had the legs, ears and horns of a goat and the body and head of a man. As god of so many things and with such a mixture of a body, it is not surprising that his name is the Greek word for 'everything'. Pan lived in Arcadia, a mountainous country in ancient Greece, and there he made the 'pan-pipes' out of reeds. Though he seems such a happy god, his appearance to travellers caused them great terror or 'panic'.

What was the Trojan Horse?

It is difficult to tell what is the truth about the Trojan War and what is the invention of story-tellers. But we do know that there was a city called Troy in what is now Turkey, and that it was the scene of a great battle in about 1230 B.C.

According to the story, the war had started ten years before this, when Paris, the son of the King of Troy, stole Helen, the beautiful wife of King Menelaus of Sparta, and took her home with him. Menelaus' brother, the great King Agamemnon of Argos, summoned all the other kings of Greek cities, and set off with a thousand ships to bring her back. For ten years the Greeks besieged Troy, without success. Then they entered the city by a trick.

They built a great wooden horse, and left it outside the city walls and went away. The Trojans thought the Greeks had gone for ever, and that the horse was a present for the gods, so they brought it inside the city. What they did not know was that the horse was full of Greek soldiers, who burst out in the middle of the night and let in the rest of the Greek army. They killed all the Trojans they could find, and set fire to the city, which was completely destroyed.

The story of the Trojan War was the subject of a famous poem by the blind Greek poet, Homer, which is called *The Iliad*. Ilium is another name for Troy.

What was the Reformation?

In the early 1500s there was a revolt against the Roman Catholic Church. Certain religious thinkers wanted the church to revise some of its out-dated ideas and stop bad practices which had grown up over the years. Though some of the men who led the demands for reform stayed loyal to the Roman Catholic Church, and never left it, others became leaders of a separate Christian movement known as Protestantism. Protestantism now has more than 200 million followers all over the world.

The movement against the ideas of the Roman Catholic Church, and the spread of Protestantism, is called the Reformation.

The Reformation came about, not just as a religious quarrel, but as a result of several things which happened at the same time. The Renaissance, aided by the invention of printing, was causing the spread of new ideas. Schools and universities were being founded in large numbers and learning was no longer confined to priests and nobles.

The Roman Catholic Church itself was weakened by struggles inside and outside. The rulers of Europe were envious of the wealth and political power of the church and the Holy Roman Empire. The old system of feudalism was breaking down and the new rising middle class of merchants and businessmen was on the side of the rulers and nobles rather than the church.

Early demands for reform came from men like Desiderius Erasmus (1466—1536), a Dutch scholar. This made him unpopular with the church authorities, although Erasmus believed strongly that the church should not be divided.

In Germany, a monk named Martin Luther (1483—1546) began a movement to stop abuses within the church such as the sale of indulgences, whereby people could pay not to be punished for forgiven sins. From 1517 Luther spoke out against the church, and in 1521 he was excommunicated, or expelled, from the church by the Pope. Luther was protected, however, by German princes who were adopting his ideas in an attempt to gain political freedom from the Holy Roman Empire.

He set up the Lutheran Church in 1522, and its influence spread rapidly through Germany, the Netherlands and part of Switzerland. Luther's support of the princes against the peasants in the Peasants' War of 1524 and 1525, however, caused many peasants to go back to Catholicism. The Lutheran church today, as well as being the oldest, is the largest Protestant Church.

In Switzerland, a priest named Huldreich Zwingli began spreading ideas much like Luther's. He was followed by John Calvin, a Frenchman, whose preachings influenced many people. Calvinism spread from Switzerland to Germany, France, the Netherlands England, and Scotland. In Scotland, the Reformation was led by John Knox, a follower of Calvin.

In England, Henry VIII quarrelled with the Pope, who would not allow him to divorce his wife, Catherine of Aragon. In 1534 Henry declared himself head of the Roman Catholic Church in England. From then on, Protestantism gradually gained ground, later — under Queen Elizabeth I — in the form of *Anglicanism*.

So Protestantism spread until it became, in its different forms, the main religion of North-Western Europe and North America, where it was taken by the Puritans.

Today there is a move towards the re-uniting of the Protestant and the Roman Catholic Churches. If, and when, this happens, perhaps the breach which began 450 years ago will finally be healed.

21ST APRIL

What was the Delphic Oracle?

In ancient times, people used to ask for advice about all kinds of important matters and expect their gods to answer, either with signs, in a dream, or through a priest.

The word 'oracle' means either a holy place where questions could be asked, or, sometimes, the answer itself. The most famous oracle was that of the Greek god

Apollo, at Delphi, high on the slopes of a sinister mountain called Parnassus.

Delphi was thought to be at the centre of the earth. Here a woman called the Pythia would sit on a tripod, or three-legged stool, and make strange noises, supposed to be inspired by the god, which were interpreted by priests. In fact, the woman was probably put into a dazed state by drugs or hypnotism, and the answers were given by the priests. They were able to collect a great deal of information because people came to Delphi from all over the world, and they were able to give sensible answers to questions like 'Where should we found a colony?'

The oracle came to be distrusted by the Greeks after it advised them against fighting the Persians, whom the Greeks in fact defeated, but it was not closed down till A.D. 390, by one of the Roman Emperors.

How does a fish breathe in the water?

Like land animals, a fish needs oxygen to live. There is plenty of oxygen dissolved in water, and the fish takes it from the water by means of its gills. The gills are feathery fronds of tissue, well supplied with blood vessels, on either side of the throat. To breathe, the fish takes in water through its mouth, then closes its mouth and squeezes the water over its gills. The blood vessels take out the oxygen and put back into the water the waste carbon dioxide gas. The water then flows out of the gill slits, which you can see on the sides of the fish's head where its neck would be if it had one. The process is the same one that goes on in our own lungs except that, because the fish lives in water, it does not have to enclose its breathing apparatus to keep it moist.

Which famous English poet was born on St George's Day?

April 23rd is one of the most significant dates in the English calendar. It is St George's Day, and St George has been the patron saint of England since the fifteenth century. Even before that he was the patron saint of the Order of the Garter, the highest order of chivalry in England. The story of how St George killed the dragon to save a beautiful princess is obviously legend. The real St George was a Christian soldier who was martyred in Palestine in about A.D. 300.

England's most famous poet and playwright, William Shakespeare, was born on April 23rd, 1564, at Stratford-on-Avon, in a house which is still standing.

He wrote most of his famous plays in London, where he was an actor in the old Globe Theatre. Several of his plays were first performed on special occasions at the courts of Queen Elizabeth and James I. He died at Stratford, also on April 23rd, in 1616.

24TH APRIL

What does Good Friday mean?

On Good Friday we remember the crucifixion of Jesus Christ. It was on Friday in the Jewish Passover week that Jesus, after being hastily tried, was taken outside the walls of Jerusalem and nailed to one of three crosses which stood on a hill called Calvary. Two thieves were crucified on the other crosses. After his death, the body was placed in a rock tomb belonging to Joseph of Arimathaea. On the third day afterwards, which we call Easter Sunday, Jesus rose from the dead.

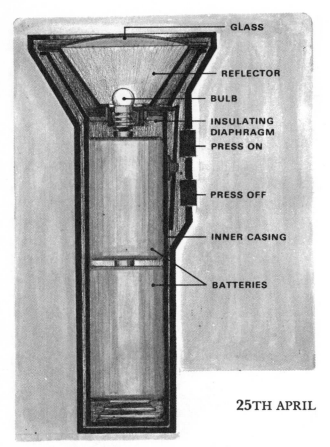

GLASS

REFLECTOR

BULB

INSULATING
DIAPHRAGM

PRESS ON

PRESS OFF

INNER CASING

BATTERIES

How does a torch work?

An electric torch consists of four main parts: the battery, the bulb, the case and the switch. The battery contains the electricity, which cannot reach the bulb until the switch is moved to connect the two.

Like all electrical equipment, the torch works by connecting the positive and negative contacts of the electrical supply, so that the current runs out at the positive contact, through the bulb and back in at the negative contact, so making a complete circuit.

When the switch is moved to the 'on' position, a piece of metal inside the case touches the positive contact of the battery, letting the electricity flow out to the bulb. In some types of torches the battery is pushed up so that the positive contact touches the bulb itself.

Who was Confucius?

Confucius, or K'ung Fu-tzu (550—479 B.C.) taught that if people would treat each other as they would like to be treated themselves, everybody would be happier. For more than two thousand years, his teaching was the state religion of China.

He founded a school where he taught his beliefs, but what he really wanted to do was become an adviser to a prince, for he believed that with the example of a good ruler, people would themselves become good. When he was made governor of the town of Chung-tu, he put his theory into practice, and people did in fact treat each other with greater courtesy and honesty.

Confucius lived to be an old man. He wrote little himself, but he was always surrounded by his pupils, and it is through their writings that we know of his sayings.

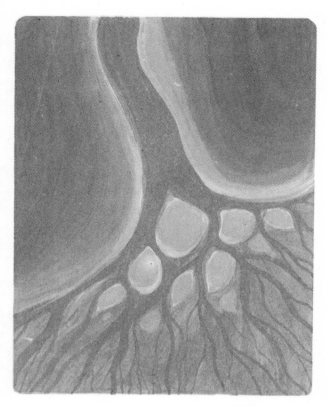

27TH APRIL

Where does cocoa come from?

We get our cocoa from the beans of the cacao tree, which was once found only in South America, but is now grown in quantity in Africa.

To make cocoa, the beans are first roasted and then ground. In the grinding they turn into a thick liquid, because half the cocoa bean consists of an oil called cocoa butter. The oil is separated and taken away to have chocolate made from it, while the fine grains which remain are the cocoa we take as a drink. Cocoa is very good for you: it is one of the most nourishing drinks you can have.

What is a delta?

A long river collects a lot of silt on its winding journey through the land. When the river reaches flat land near the sea it becomes slow and broad. And the silt — which is made up of sand, soil and decaying vegetable matter — sinks to the bottom. In time the silt fills up the river bed and causes the water to spread further over the land, splitting up into many different streams. All of these streams go on dropping silt until a broad plain is built up. The plain, with the streams branching out on their different ways to the sea is called a delta. The word comes from the Greek letter delta, or D, which is shaped like a triangle. Typical deltas are those of the Nile, the Amazon and the Mississippi.

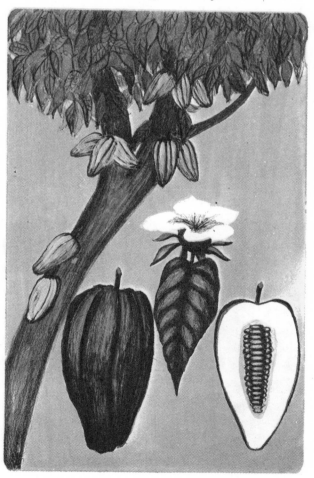

Is lightning dangerous?

A flash of lightning is a great discharge of natural electricity which can look very frightening during a bad storm. In the ordinary way of things it is not dangerous: most lightning flashes do not even reach the ground. However, from time to time it shows its power by blasting a tree, smashing off a chimney pot, or even by killing somebody.

Most people who are killed by lightning happen to be sheltering under a tree at the time. This is the most dangerous thing to do during a thunderstorm. Trees and tall buildings help lightning to strike down to the ground. Most buildings are fitted with lightning conductors: metal strips which guide the electricity safely down. But a tree is one big lightning conductor and the electricity burns right down the bark, often leaving a charred gash from top to bottom. Anybody standing under the tree is in great danger of being electrocuted.

So the answer is that lightning is not often dangerous — but do not take chances.

30TH APRIL

Which country is the home of the kangaroo?

Australia is the home of the most primitive mammals in the world. Millions of years ago, when certain reptiles were turning into the first mammals, the marsupials — or pouched mammals — emerged. As more advanced mammals came into being, the marsupials over the rest of the world — save for the American opossum — were killed and became extinct. But in Australia, cut off from Asia when seas swept away the land bridge, the marsupials survived. And today they are still there: the kangaroo, the wallaby, the koala bear and the opossum.

Marsupials are such primitive mammals that they *almost* lay eggs. What happens instead is that the young are born alive, but not properly formed. The baby of the kangaroo is only 25 millimetres long at birth. Some blind instinct makes it climb up its mother's fur and into the pouch. It spends six months in there, feeding on its mother's milk and growing into a normal baby. The same thing happens with the other marsupials.

The kangaroo multiplied in Australia until its numbers threatened the grasslands of the sheep farmers. Since then its numbers have been kept down.

What is the meaning of May?

The goddess Maia gave her name to the month of May. She was not a very famous goddess, but she had a famous father, Atlas, who was supposed to carry the world on his shoulders, and a famous son, Hermes.

In mediaeval times, May 1st was celebrated in England by crowning a May Queen and dancing round a May-pole.

Since 1889, May Day has also been significant, especially in Communist countries, as an international holiday.

What was the earliest clock?

The earliest way of telling the time was by marking the progress of the shadow cast by a twig stuck upright in the ground. Round about 1300 B.C. this was developed by the inhabitants of ancient Egypt and Mesopotamia into the sundial.

The sundial served for a thousand years until the invention of the *clepsydra,* or water clock. This was the first clock with moving parts. Water dripped into a cylinder and caused a floating piston to rise. This piston worked a ratchet which turned the single hand, the hour hand, of the clock.

The mechanical clock was not invented until the thirteenth century, and then it was driven by weights. This meant clocks were of great size and could not be carried about. The spring-driven clock was invented about 1450.

2ND MAY

How can ice burn you?

The burning sensation you get when you touch something hot, say a hot poker, is caused by the effect of the heat on the nerve-endings in your fingers. These nerve-endings flash a message to the brain, in the form of a stab of pain, that says something dangerous is happening to the fingers. The brain flashes a message back to tell the fingers to drop the poker.

In the same way you can get a burning sensation by holding your hand against a block of ice. It is not so severe as the pain caused by something hot, but it is very similar in feeling, and is caused by the body's heat being suddenly taken away from the nerve-endings. The burning feeling lingers on in both cases because the sensitive nerve-endings have been damaged by the sudden change in temperature.

4TH MAY

What is chromium?

Chromium, discovered by Vauquelin, a French chemist, in 1797, is a silvery metal which does not rust. For this reason, it is used to protect metals which otherwise corrode. Sometimes it is used as a coating: the process called *chromium-plating* puts a thin skin of chrome on metal objects. In other processes it is mixed with the metal during smelting: stainless steel, for instance, is made by mixing chromium with the ordinary steel. The result is a steel which does not rust.

What is a mirage?

Have you ever looked along a smooth road in hot weather and seen what appears to be a stretch of water where none exists? This is a mirage. It is caused by the air being heated in such a way that hot layers of air lie under cold layers. The cold air is thicker than the hot air and this causes light passing through the layers to be bent. This bending gives the illusion of water, or even sends a picture of the scene many miles away.

Mirages often occur in the desert. Lakes are seen where there is really nothing but sand. And sometimes images of towns and palm trees appear and taunt the thirsty traveller. The same thing happens at sea, when ghostly ships are seen floating in the sky.

It is easy to tell a mirage from the real thing, however, because the objects in it are all upside down. This is caused by the way the rays of light are bent.

What are vitamins?

Vitamins are chemicals which our bodies must have if they are to grow and function properly. There are many vitamins, found in various foods, and each helps us in different ways. They were discovered in 1912, and named after letters of the alphabet, but long before then, people knew that certain foods were necessary to stop certain bodily disorders. In 1601, for instance, it was discovered that the juice of limes prevented scurvy. This disease was common in the navy because of the lack of fresh vegetables on long voyages, and in 1795 limes were made a regular part of the sailor's diet. The limes contained ascorbic acid, or Vitamin C, which is found in green vegetables and certain fruits.

Vitamin A, which helps growth, is found in cod liver oil, milk, butter and eggs, carrots and tomatoes. Vitamin D helps young bones to grow strong and is found also in cod-liver oil, milk and butter. This vitamin can also be formed by our own bodies from sunshine.

Our bodies need only small quantities of these vitamins, but they cannot store them. It would be of no use at all to drink a pint of cod-liver oil and expect to have enough Vitamin A to last the year. So vitamins have to be taken regularly, and the best way of doing this is to eat a varied diet.

Why does a beaver build a dam?

There are two kinds of beaver, the European and the American. The European beaver, which is found in France, Poland and Norway, lives in burrows, but the American beaver builds a home of branches and mud called a 'lodge'.

He builds the lodge in a lake or stream, so that he can have the entrance underwater, safe from his enemies. If the site for his home is in a swift, shallow stream, he builds a dam of tree trunks which he gnaws down with his chisel-like teeth and floats to the spot he has chosen. The water builds up behind the dam to form a deep, calm pond and the beaver has an ideal place for a home.

7TH MAY

Who lives at Buckingham Palace?

Buckingham Palace, built in 1703 for the Duke of Buckingham, has been the home of the British royal family since it was bought by George III in 1761.

In it today live Queen Elizabeth II, her husband, Prince Philip, Prince Andrew and Prince Edward. The railings at the front of the Palace are almost always thronged with visitors, either hoping to catch a glimpse of the royal family or content to watch the marching of the Guards on sentry-go. The Guards used to do sentry duty outside the railings, but a few years ago the press of visitors became so great that they moved inside.

9TH MAY

25,000 people. And it takes 1,000 people just to look after the building, to sweep, polish, repair it and clean the 6,500 windows.

The tallest building in Britain, the 188-metre-high GPO Exchange Tower in London is tiny by Comparison.

Architects are now working on a method of construction which will allow buildings to soar much higher.

10TH MAY

Which is the world's highest building?

The finest collection of the world's tall buildings are the skyscrapers of New York. One of them, the Empire State, is the tallest inhabited building in the world: 448 metres to the top of the television tower which caps it.

The Empire State has 102 storeys, and if you want to walk up, you will have to climb 1,860 steps. Most people very sensibly prefer to take one of the 63 passenger lifts. Inside the building are the offices of 940 firms, which between them employ

What is a caterpillar?

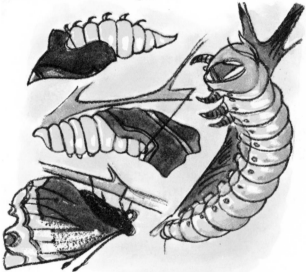

You may have seen caterpillars in the garden, perhaps eating up your father's cabbages, and found it very hard to believe that these clumsy creatures can turn into the delicate butterflies that you see in the summer. The caterpillar, in fact, is just a stage in the development of the family of *lepidoptera* — butterflies and moths.

First an egg is laid, usually on some kind of leaf, and this hatches into a *larva*, or caterpillar, which feeds on the leaf, until it is ready to become a chrysalis. The caterpillars are protected from other creatures in various ways. For instance, they are often very hairy, or have spikes, so that no bird could swallow them. Some can even throw out poisonous acid. The chrysalis or *pupa*, is the next stage. The pupa cannot move and makes a hard protective 'cocoon' for itself, out of silk. When it is ready to hatch, it bites its way through the cocoon and emerges as a delicate winged creature.

11TH MAY

Why is Dunkirk remembered?

In May 1940, the German Army advanced rapidly through France. The British and French armies were pushed to the sea and were finally hemmed in at a port called Dunkirk. It looked as if they would all be killed or taken prisoner, but a great fleet of a thousand ships and boats — most of them tiny private motor-boats and yachts — crossed the Channel from Britain and in the eight days from the 27th May rescued more than 300,000 soldiers.

All the time the soldiers and the ships were under heavy attack from German aircraft. This would have been even worse had not the British Air Force shot down so many German planes before they could reach the beaches.

After Dunkirk, France fell to the Germans and Britain stood alone, expecting every day to be invaded. The invasion, however, never came. For three months German planes bombed towns and cities in Britain, but suffered heavy losses from attacks by British fighters in the Battle of Britain.

We remember Dunkirk, then, for the heroic stand of the British and French, and the courage of the men in the little ships who rescued them. We remember it as the defeat out of which came victory.

Who was Garibaldi?

In the 1840s, Italy was a collection of small states, mainly under foreign rule. Naples, in the south, was linked with Spain; Venetia and Lombardy, in the north, were governed by Austria; the Pope ruled the middle, and there were four independent states, Parma, Modena, Lucca, and Tuscany. Piedmont,

12TH MAY

Who was Robin Hood?

Like many of the old English heroes, the real Robin Hood has become so mixed up with legends that it is almost impossible now to say which was which. He was an outlaw who lived with his band in Sherwood Forest, in Nottinghamshire. Some stories say he was a 'goodly yeoman', others that he was the Earl of Huntingdon. Nobody can be sure even of his name: it may have been Robin Hood, Rob o' th' Hood (from his dress), or Rob in th' Wood (from his hiding place). Whatever the truth about Robin, the stories of his robbing the rich to give to the poor, in the company of Maid Marian, Little John, Friar Tuck and the rest of his merry men, are still exciting.

in the north-west, was part of Sardinia.

Many people hoped to win Italy for the Italians, but while most of them just talked about it, or made feeble protests, a fiery soldier, called Guiseppe Garibaldi, refused to be kept down. With a band of volunteers, known as 'Red-shirts', he fought a series of battles with the outsiders.

In 1860, he conquered Sicily and Naples and marched north. Meanwhile, King Victor Emmanuel of Sardinia was marching south. When they met, Garibaldi hailed him as the first king of a united Italy.

14TH MAY

What is silk made of?

Several insects and spiders produce silk (a spider's web is made from it) but the silk we wear is made from the cocoon of a caterpillar with the long name of *Bombyx-mori*. It is easier to call it by its common name of 'silkworm'.

This caterpillar, the larva of the flightless silk moth, feeds greedily on mulberry leaves until the time comes to make a chrysalis. Then a cocoon is spun from up to 900 metres of fine gossamer thread, which is squirted out as a liquid from an opening in its bottom lip, hardening as it comes in contact with the air. It is wound round and round the chrysalis. To make silken thread strong enough to be woven into cloth, four or more of these strands are twisted together.

Silk has been prized by man for thousands of years (for 3,000 years the arts of spinning and weaving it were kept secret by the Chinese). Today it is produced in great quantities in Japan, China, Italy and France.

15TH MAY

What is blood?

Blood is the fluid which flows through our bodies. It carries nourishment and oxygen to our organs and muscles, and takes away waste matter. An adult human has about 4.5 litres of blood in his body, constantly being pumped round by the heart.

Blood is made up of a liquid called *plasma* and red and white cells called *corpuscles*. Plasma is a yellowish fluid which has dissolved in it several chemicals which our bodies need. There are two kinds of corpuscles, red and white. The red ones carry a substance called *haemoglobin*, and it is this which carries oxygen from the lungs to wherever it is needed in the body. The white cells — there is only one of these to every five hundred red ones — are our bodies' policemen. They fight any germs they come across and also carry away waste matter.

Scientists have classified blood into four main groups (A, B, AB and O). Nowadays

if anyone is so badly hurt as to need a blood transfusion, the doctors can find out his group and make sure he gets the right kind. This is very important, because blood from different groups will not work together.

16TH MAY

What is an iceberg?

An iceberg is a great mass of floating ice which has broken off either from the end of a glacier or from one of the great ice-sheets of the polar regions.

Some icebergs are of enormous size and, as only a ninth part shows above the water, they can be very dangerous to shipping. Icebergs sticking up 90 metres from the waves have been seen in Arctic waters. This means that beneath the surface they would go down another 720 metres.

The biggest disaster caused by an iceberg was the sinking of the *Titanic*. On her first voyage in 1912 the great liner struck an iceberg in the Atlantic and sank with the loss of 1,513 lives. Previously, it had been thought that the Titanic was unsinkable.

Since then, a watch has been kept on icebergs by the International Ice Patrol, which warns of any 'bergs which drift into shipping lanes.

Which are the principal oceans of the world?

We tend to think of the world as being stretches of land separated by water. What the surface of the world really is, however, is one great stretch of water broken up in places by land. Seven-tenths of the world is covered by the five great oceans which all flow into one another.

The largest ocean is the *Pacific,* dotted with many tiny islands. The *Atlantic,* which separates the American continent from Europe and Africa, is narrower. The *Indian Ocean,* as its name suggests, is the ocean into which India sticks out from the Asian land mass. The *Arctic Ocean* is the one around the North Pole, and the *Southern Ocean* is the one around the South Pole.

What is the Order of the Golden Fleece?

The Order of the Golden Fleece is a knightly order founded by Duke Philip of Burgundy in 1430. In the sixteenth century, the House of Burgundy was merged with the Hapsburg family, who governed Spain and Austria, and the Golden Fleece became the chief order of knighthood in both countries, and the most famous continental order. It was abolished in Austria after World War I, but still exists as Spain's most prized award.

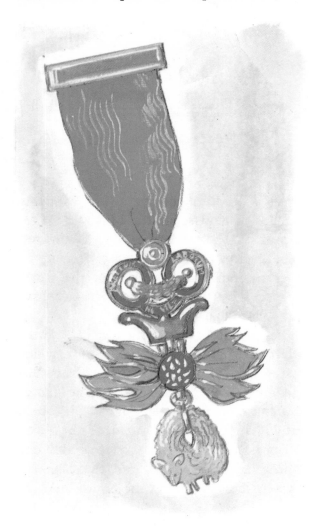

What is a prophet?

A prophet is someone who has the power to see into the future and to tell other people what lies ahead. Others can make prophecies simply by studying things which are already known, and working out from them the things which are likely to happen. Some people claim to be able to foretell the future by the study of the stars, and in this way they can claim to be prophets.

Many of the famous prophets of old, such as those in the Hebrew scriptures, were religious prophets: that is, they were inspired by God to warn and teach.

What is a quarry?

A quarry is an open pit dug in the ground so that rock or sand can be easily taken out. The best place for a quarry is on the side of a hill so that the rock can be cut out in steps and taken away without having to be hauled up to the top. Slate and marble are examples of rocks cut out from quarries. Often the rocks are blown out by explosives.

Sometimes coal can be got by removing all the earth on top of the seam, instead of sinking a narrow shaft down to it. This method, which is called 'opencast' mining, is really a form of quarrying.

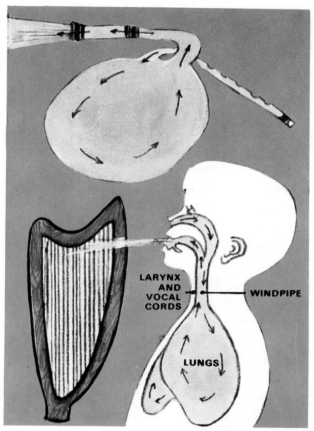

LARYNX AND VOCAL CORDS

WINDPIPE

LUNGS

21ST MAY

How does a person speak?

Many parts of our body go into the making of the sounds which we utter and the words which we say to one another. Speech starts when the diaphragm squeezes air out of our lungs and into the windpipe. At the top end of the windpipe is the *larynx*, or 'Adam's apple' — that is the hard bit you can feel at the front of your neck. Inside the larynx are the vocal cords, two bands of elastic tissue like the strings of a violin. As the air passes over these cords, they vibrate to produce sound.

Sound is turned into words when it reaches the mouth, by movements of the tongue and lips.

91

What is soap made of?

You can buy all kinds of soap, in all colours and smelling of many different and pleasant things. All these soaps, however, are a mixture of animal or vegetable oils and fats, and caustic soda or caustic potash. The fats, such as tallow or coconut oil, are boiled together with the soda or potash and allowed to harden.

Soap was known centuries before Christ, though in Europe it was not made in any quantity for a long time after that. The first soap factory in England was set up in Bristol in the twelfth century.

We get dirty because the grease on our skin makes the dirt cling. Soap gets the dirt off because it turns this grease into something that will mix easily with water.

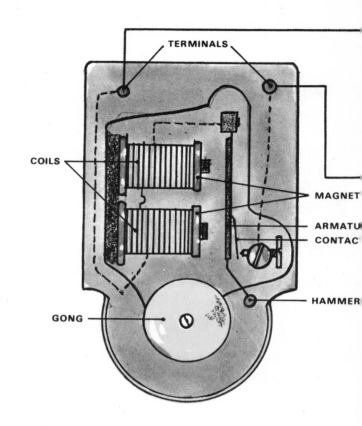

TERMINALS
COILS
MAGNET
ARMATU
CONTAC
HAMMER
GONG

What is electricity?

Each of the 103 elements from which everything in the world is made is composed of atoms. Round these atoms, at speeds impossible to imagine, circle *electrons*. It is the movement of these electrons which is the mysterious force we call electricity.

An electric current is caused by the jumping of an electron from one atom to another. Each atom can have only a fixed number of electrons, so the atom which gets the extra electron immediately passes one on to the next atom, and so on, through countless millions of atoms so long as there are atoms to gain and lose electrons.

You can get some idea of the process by

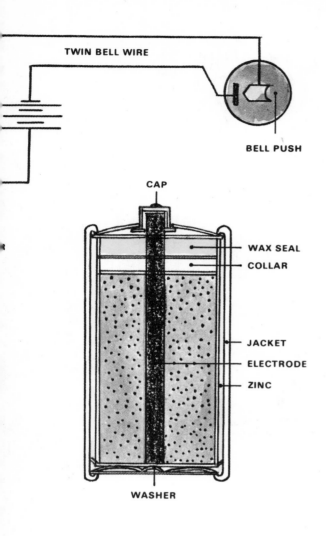

TWIN BELL WIRE

BELL PUSH

CAP

WAX SEAL

COLLAR

JACKET

ELECTRODE

ZINC

WASHER

24TH MAY

What is a seahorse?

rolling a marble to hit the end of a line of marbles. Each marble knocks its neighbour, right the way down the line, until the end marble rolls away, knocked by the marble before it and having no other marble to pass the energy on to.

Nature is full of electricity, from the static electricity in the fur of a cat, caused by the friction of the hairs, to the great and terrible power of a flash of lightning. Man has learned to make electricity in two ways: by chemical action, as in a battery, and by moving loops of wire between magnets, as in a dynamo, to set up an electric current in the wire.

The strange seahorse, though it looks sometimes like a little hobby-horse, sometimes like a tiny dragon, is a fish. It is a member of the family of pipe fishes and, like its relatives, has a bony body.

It swims upright among the clumps of seaweed in which it lives, propelling itself by the solitary back fin. It has no tail fins: it uses its tail to coil around the seaweed when it wants to rest. The seahorse — there are fifty different varieties — prefers warm, shallow water and lives in tropical or warm seas. It is found in the Mediterranean and the sunnier parts of the Atlantic. When the eggs are laid, they are taken over by the father fish and put in a little pouch near his tail. There they stay until they hatch.

93

What gives us energy?

For our bodies to grow and work properly, we must have a properly-balanced diet. As well as vitamins and certain minerals, which we get from vegetables and water, what we need are proteins, carbohydrates and fats.

Proteins — which are provided by eggs, milk, lean meat and certain vegetables — are what our bodies use for building bone and muscle.

Carbohydrates and fats are what we turn into energy to use in running, jumping, walking, swimming, skipping — or even thinking. Sugar and starch are the main carbohydrates, and we get them from sugar itself, from potatoes, and from cereals — corn, oats, wheat and barley — and the things made from them, like bread. Fats we get from butter, meat and vegetable oils.

How is cheese made?

Cheese has been known to man for almost 3,500 years as a very nourishing form of food which is easy to store and carry about.

It is made from the fat and casein, a protein substance, from milk. First of all lactic acid and rennet (a substance taken from the stomach of a calf) are added to the milk. This curdles the milk and makes the fat and casein stick together. The water, or whey, is poured off, and what is left is pressed together and left to ripen. There are many kinds of cheeses, some hard, some soft, some creamy, and how they turn out depends on how they are made, how much water is left in, and how they are cured.

What is an avalanche?

An avalanche is the fall of large masses of snow, ice, earth or rocks, from a mountain slope down into the valley below. Avalanches of snow are the most common: every year comes news of them from mountainous countries like Switzerland. The mountain sides become so piled up with snow that an extra fall gives just enough weight to bring the whole lot down. Even a loud noise, like a gunshot, can bring down tonnes of snow. Ice avalanches occur when great pieces of ice break off from the end of a glacier and tumble further down the valley.

28TH MAY

What is heraldry?

When men began to band together in families and tribes, they found it useful to have a mark or a symbol to show which one they belonged to. In battle the use of this symbol on a shield or banner was of great help in showing which side was which.

This happened all over the world and was the beginnings of heraldry. The Roman eagle, badge of Imperial Rome, was a heraldic emblem, acting as a rallying point to the soldiers in the thick of the fray. Richard I, the famous Lionheart, used a lion as his symbol, on banner and shield.

As more people began to use badges and coats of arms, certain colours for these became agreed on, and animals were given certain positions with special heraldic names: *rampant* (rearing up), *passant* (prowling) or *couchant* (sleeping).

In England, for hundreds of years the College of Heralds has decided who shall have a coat-of-arms, and also has to agree on the form it takes.

Are all snowflakes exactly alike?

A snowflake is formed when water vapour in the air suddenly freezes, turning from gas to solid without having time to turn liquid in between. This results in a six-rayed crystal of delicate and wonderful beauty. Countless millions of these crystals make up even a light fall of snow — many of them cling together to fall as large 'flakes' — but it would be hard to find any two exactly alike. The snowflake is a marvellous example of nature's habit of setting a pattern and then letting every substance make its own little variation on it.

Who was Joan of Arc?

Joan of Arc, or Jeanne d'Arc, was a peasant girl who led the French to victory against the English and Burgundians in 1428. The French were faring badly in the war, but Joan, after seeing visions and hearing heavenly voices, asked the king for a troop of soldiers. Led by Joan, these soldiers broke the English siege of Orleans and cleared the surrounding countryside. Then, in 1430, Joan tried to recapture Paris, but she was taken by the Burgundians and sold to the English, who accused her of witchcraft, tried and condemned her, and burned her at the stake in Rouen market place on May 30th, 1431. She was declared a saint in 1920.

What is a knight?

Knighthood is an honour conferred by a king or his representatives. In feudal times, knights were expected to give service to the king in war, and take with them their own servants from their lands. In the later middle ages, knighthood became more like a monastic creation, and developed a code of good behaviour, which was called chivalry. Some orders of knighthood in fact, like the Knights Templar and the Knights of St John of Jerusalem, were originally wholly religious foundations, until they were forced to use arms in self-defence. In Britain today, there are two kinds of knights, knights bachelor, who are just knights, and knights of the various orders — like the Orders of the Garter, the Thistle and the Bath.

When the Queen knights someone, she 'dubs' him, by tapping the sword of state on each shoulder, then she commands 'Rise, Sir . . .' and says his Christian name. His wife can call herself Lady . . ., with her surname. The title cannot be passed from a man to his son.

What is the meaning of June?

The fact that we get the names of our months from the Romans has led to arguments over the meaning of June. Some people think it was named after an old Roman family called Junius, but it is more likely that it was after the goddess Juno, the wife of Jupiter and queen of heaven, who rode about in a chariot drawn by peacocks. In ancient Rome, a festival was celebrated in her honour at the beginning of the month.

Why does iron rust?

Some metals are easily affected by the oxygen in the air, and combine with it to form an *oxide*. Iron is one of these: in water, or damp surroundings, it forms the oxide we know as rust. (*Hydrated ferric oxide* is its full title). Iron does not rust in dry air, nor does it rust in water which is free from acid. This means that rusting needs the combined action of air, water and acid. However, as there is always plenty of carbonic acid in the air and in rainwater, it is easy to see why you should not leave your garden fork out overnight.

2ND JUNE

What is charcoal?

Charcoal is a form of carbon made by heating wood while at the same time keeping the air out. Charcoal burns with a fierce heat and was used a great deal in the early days of the iron industry. Nowadays it is made in steel furnaces, but at one time the cone-shaped heaps of logs, covered by turf or clay to keep out the air, were a common sight in the forests. When the iron industry led to a great demand for charcoal, whole forests were destroyed to provide it.

Charcoal has many other uses besides providing heat: it is used for purifying and filtering liquids and gases, and by artists for drawing.

Which birds do not fly?

The birds which do not fly gave up the use of their wings many thousands of years ago simply because they did not need them. They either lived in places where there were no dangerous animals to hunt them, or were so big that they could rely on their legs to carry them out of trouble.

The penguin, as you have read, turned his wings into paddles. The kiwi of New Zealand took to living by night, finding his food by smell. Not only did he not need his wings — he did not need his eyes, either, and nowadays he has very poor sight. The most ferocious flightless bird is the cassowary, who lives in the jungles of Indonesia. He fears neither man nor beast and is quick to attack with the talons on his long legs.

The biggest flightless bird in the world is the African ostrich. Growing to 2.5 metres tall, he can run across open desert at forty miles an hour, covering 4.5 metres in one stride! The next biggest is the Australian emu, a bird much like the cassowary but not nearly so fierce. In South America lives the rhea, which looks like a smaller and prettier ostrich. The poor rheas were hunted down in thousands when feathers were in demand for hats and fans during the last century.

When a letter is posted, what happens to it?

The delivery of a letter the day after it was posted, perhaps at the other end of the country, is something we take for granted. Only when a letter is late in arriving do we perhaps stop to think how it reached us.

Its journey begins when you drop it into a pillar box. From there it is collected with all the others by a postman, who travels round from box to box by van, and takes the letters to the nearest GPO sorting office.

Here they have the postmark put on them by franking machines. Then they are sorted. Those for areas round about are sorted into towns, villages and streets. Those for distant parts of the country are left roughly sorted out into areas and then put on a train.

As the train travels through the night, sorters work in a specially-equipped carriage. Mail trains can pick up and put down mail without even stopping. A net which sticks out from the carriage scoops up a mail bag hung from a frame on the station platform. At the same time, a bag of mail for that town is dropped from the train into a net on the ground.

Letters brought by the mail train go to the post office at their destination for the final 'fine' sorting into streets, and are then given to the postman for delivery. Off he sets, in hail, rain, snow, fog or flood, to make sure you get the letter you have been waiting for so anxiously.

What happened on D-Day?

During the Second World War, on the 6th June, 1944, British and American troops crossed the Channel to win back France from the Germans. About 116,000 soldiers landed in Normandy in the biggest air and sea-borne invasion ever made. The actual day of landing was a secret, and was always referred to as 'D-Day'.

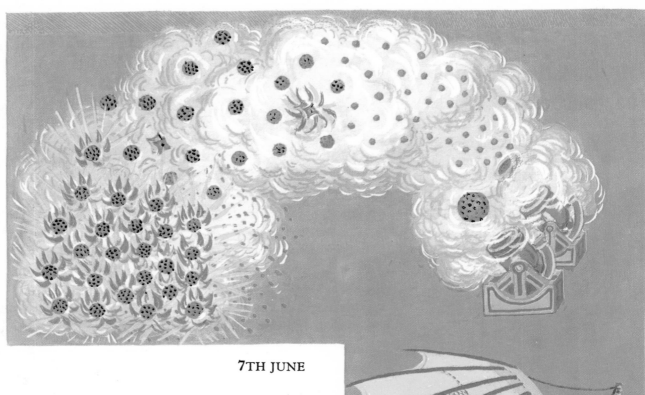

What is Leonardo da Vinci remembered for, apart from his paintings?

The Italian Leonardo da Vinci (1452—1519) produced many drawings, paintings (including the Mona Lisa) and statues. And he seems to have found time to do almost everything else. He was a mathematician, an architect and an engineer. He made many discoveries about light, heat, and friction. He produced theories about the movement of the earth and started the classification of animals into vertebrates and invertebrates. He also invented many things, not all of which worked. His inventions were far ahead of his time: one of them, for instance, was for a flying machine very much like our modern helicopter and another was for an armoured fighting machine like the tank.

Why is the sea salt?

When rain falls on the land it dissolves particles of salt in soil and rocks. The rainwater runs into streams, the streams run into rivers and the rivers — carrying the salt — run into the sea. The water is warmed by the sun, turns into vapour, and falls again on the land as rain. But the salt stays behind in the sea. Over millions of years enough of it has collected there for us to be able to taste it.

10TH JUNE

What does SOS mean?

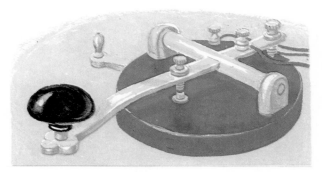

SOS is the Morse code signal used by ships of all countries to show that they are in distress. Many explanations have been given for the letters: you may have heard people say that they mean 'Save Our Souls' or 'Send Our Succour'. But really they have no meaning: they are used because in Morse code they are easy to transmit and easy to recognise. The code is three dots, three dashes, three dots . . . — — — . . . Try it. Either tap it, or flash it with a torch.

8TH JUNE

Why do some trees lose their leaves in the winter?

Trees go to sleep for the winter. They stop growing and the movement of sap slows right down. When a tree is in this state its leaves are of no use to it: in fact they could be a nuisance. There is not enough sap to feed them and they would be badly damaged by frost. Part of the job of the leaves is to make food for the tree from sunlight, water and a gas called carbon dioxide. In winter, however, there is not enough sunlight to make this worthwhile, so many trees — the ones we call deciduous — drop their leaves until the warm weather comes again.

What is poison?

A poison is anything which, when taken in sufficient quantity, is able to make us ill or even kill us. Many chemicals are poisonous: prussic acid and strychnine, for instance, can kill in very small doses. Other chemicals which we take as medicine can become poisonous if we have too much of them. It is possible also to be poisoned by food. Some fungi, like toadstools, and berries like those of the 'deadly' nightshade, are very dangerous things to eat. Even meat and fish can be poisonous if they are not fresh. The danger here comes from the germs which are living in the decaying tissues.

What is the festival of Corpus Christi?

Since the middle of the fourteenth century, one of the most important and colourful religious festivals celebrated in Roman Catholic countries has been the feast of *Corpus Christi*, on the Thursday after Trinity Sunday. The words mean 'the body of Christ', and the feast celebrates the presence of Christ in the Sacrament, which is carried through the town in procession.

In different places, different customs have grown up. Usually, the important men in the town appear in their official robes. Sometimes, as in Orvieto in Italy, people dress up in historical costumes, or, as in Campobasso, as characters from the Old and New Testaments. In Granada, in Spain, celebrations go on for a week.

What was the Magna Carta?

King John of England was a bad ruler. He taxed people heavily, put others in prison without trial and did all sorts of things that made him unpopular. So in 1215, the barons and bishops got together and made John put his seal (he could not write!) on the *Magna Carta,* which means 'the Great Charter', at a ceremony in the meadow of Runnymede, by the Thames. He had to agree, because without their soldiers and their money, he would not be able to rule at all.

The Magna Carta was a statement of the law and a guarantee of certain rights and freedoms. Though it is often hailed as a great document of English freedom, it really only helped the barons, the Church and the merchants. However, it was a beginning, and over the centuries the freedoms of ordinary people have grown into those we enjoy today.

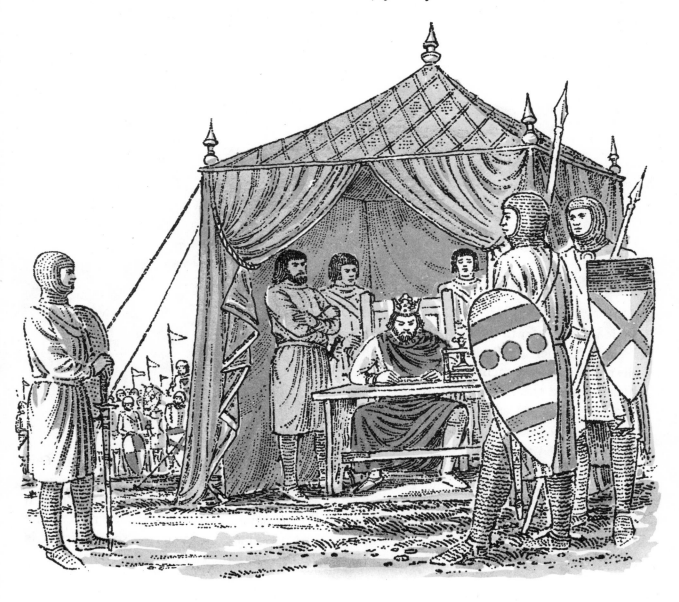

Althing meets in Reykjavik, the capital of Iceland, and has two houses, an upper and a lower, which are equally powerful. One-third of the members sit in the Upper House. All people over eighteen may vote for candidates, who are usually drawn from the four main political parties on the island. Elections for the Icelandic parliament are held every four years.

15TH JUNE

Can you eat an acorn?

You can eat an acorn if you *want* to. Our ancestors used to eat them when the land was covered with great forests. The reason they stopped is that there are nuts to be had which are far tastier — so perhaps it is best to leave the acorns to the squirrels.

14TH JUNE

Which is the oldest Parliament?

People usually refer to the British Parliament as 'The Mother of Parliaments', but the oldest existing parliament is that of Iceland, which is called the *Althing*, meaning 'whole assembly'. This parliament first met in the year A.D. 930. Iceland by then had been settled for nearly sixty years by hardy Norsemen. Since 1944, the country has been a republic, and a president is elected for four years. The real running of the country however, is done by the Prime Minister and his six-man cabinet — subject, of course, to the wishes of parliament. The

What do the week days mean?

The sun and the moon give us the names of the first two days of the week: Sunday and Monday. The rest, except for Saturday, are named after the gods and goddesses of our northern ancestors. Tuesday is named after Tyr, or Tiw, the Norse god of war. Wednesday is named after Woden, the greatest of the northern gods. Thursday is the day of Thor, the thunder god. Friday comes from Freya, the wife of Woden, mother of Thor. She was given a day so that she would not be jealous. Saturday is named after the Roman god, Saturn.

107

Who won the Battle of Waterloo?

The Battle of Waterloo, which ended the Hundred Days' freedom of Napoleon Bonaparte after his escape from exile on the Isle of Elba, was fought near the village of Waterloo, in Belgium, on 18th June, 1815. On one side were British and Dutch troops under the Duke of Wellington, and Prussian troops under Marshal Blücher. On the other

17TH JUNE

Where is the sun at night?

The sun at night is in exactly the same place it was during the day. It is *we* who have moved. We get night and day because the earth spins round, once every twenty-four hours. When night falls it means that the part of the earth on which we are standing is turning away from the sun. And while we are fast asleep, someone on the other side of the earth is waking up to start a new day because his part of the earth is turning towards the sun.

were the French troops under Napoleon. Napoleon had defeated the Prussians earlier and thought he would have only the English and Dutch to deal with. But the Prussian army had recovered, and was marching to join Wellington. The British and Dutch stood firm against fierce French attacks, and when the Prussians finally arrived to help, just as night was falling, the French were beaten and driven off in disorder.

This was the final defeat of Napoleon, who had been trying to conquer Europe since 1799. He was sent to the island of St Helena, where he died in 1821.

What is a zoo?

'Zoo' is short for 'zoological gardens', which means a place where wild animals are kept so that people can see them and study them. Though animals in zoos are well fed and looked after, they are not happy if they are kept in a small cage. So many zoos nowadays are trying out new ways of keeping them so that they can roam about and feel free, even though they cannot get out. London Zoo has many fine new enclosures like this, and at Whipsnade Zoo the animals have lots of pleasant grassland to roam in.

20TH JUNE

Which British Sovereign had the longest reign?

On June 20th, 1837, an 18-year-old girl succeeded to the British throne on the death of her uncle, King William IV. Sixty-three years and seven months later in January, 1901, she died, after the longest reign of any British monarch. She was, of course, Victoria, Queen of Great Britain and Ireland, and Empress of India. Victoria's reign was eventful, as well as long. Britain during that time became more and more rich and powerful, and was busy building up a large Empire overseas. At home it was a time of great inventions and swift industrial progress.

In 1840 she married her cousin, Prince Albert of Saxe-Coburg-Gotha. How much the British people liked him can be judged from his nickname of 'Albert the Good'. When Albert died, in 1861, Queen Victoria was so distressed that she withdrew for years from all social occasions. But she was

still active in the background, and insisted that her ministers could make no important decisions without her approval, so she gave a very definite character to 'the Victorian Age'.

She had nine children, who married into the other royal families of Europe, so that most of these families are now related. The present Queen, Elizabeth II, is the great-great-granddaughter of Queen Victoria.

21ST JUNE

Who discovered radium?

The radioactive substance called radium was discovered in 1898 by Pierre and Marie Curie after they had worked together in Paris on radio-active research for only two years. Radium has been very valuable in the curing of disease and in industry.

Which is the most intelligent mammal?

By far the most intelligent of the mammals is man himself. And next to him come the apes: the chimpanzee, gorilla, gibbon and orang-utan, all of whom are descended — with man — from the same ape-like creature. Of these apes, the chimpanzee is the most intelligent. He is quick to learn, and able to solve reasonably difficult problems. In recent years, tame chimps have even produced 'paintings' which have been sold for large sums of money.

23RD JUNE

Who invented the steam engine?

Several inventors contributed ideas towards the making of the first steam engine, but the very first successful engine was made in 1698 by an Englishman named Thomas Savery. It was used for pumping water, as was the improved engine of Thomas Newcomen in 1710. Both engines, however, wasted power, and the man who made the biggest advance in the engine's design was James Watt, who brought out his steam engine in 1769. From then onwards, there was rapid advance in the use of the steam engine in industry and transport.

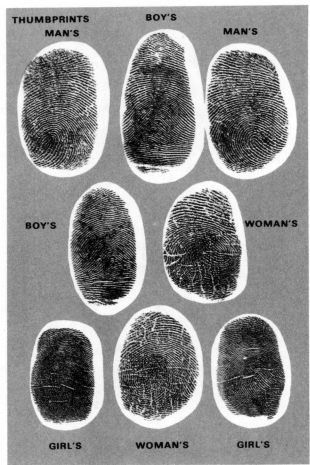

What are finger prints?

Like snowflakes, no two persons' finger prints are exactly alike, not even those of identical twins. A pattern is formed by the ridge of the skin on the tips of the fingers, and stays the same from the day of a person's birth to the day he dies. These two facts make finger prints very useful in identifying somebody beyond any mistake, and this is why police forces find them invaluable in tracking down a criminal. The largest collection of finger prints is held by the Federal Bureau of Investigation in America.

Finger prints are easily classified as there are four different basic shapes of pattern — arches, loops, whorls and composites — which are subdivided according to things like the numbers of ridges between certain points in the pattern.

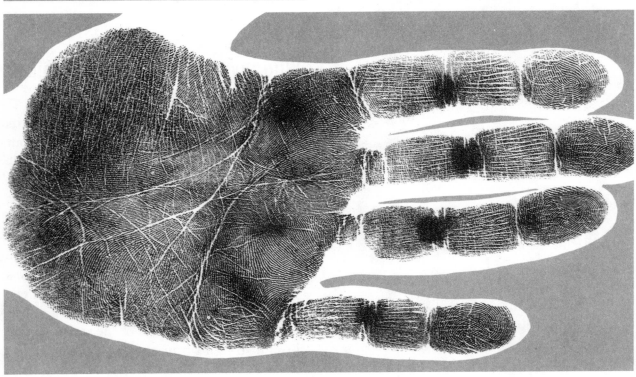

What is the Milky Way?

We had better start by describing a *galaxy*. A galaxy is a gigantic collection of stars, planets, gas and dust, which makes a slowly-turning 'island' in space. The Milky Way is the galaxy we live in, and our own solar system (the collection of planets which revolves round the sun) is only a tiny part of this galaxy.

In the Milky Way are something like a hundred thousand stars, not counting all the small planets and satellites. It is shaped like a discus — the round disc that athletes throw — with many stars clustered at the centre to make a bulge.

Though the Milky Way seems vast to us (it takes light a hundred thousand years to get from one side to the other) it is only one of millions of galaxies in the whole of the universe. The next galaxy to ours, leaving out two 'small' collections which could be regarded as satellites of the Milky Way, is Andromeda. It takes light from Andromeda *a million and half years* to reach us.

If you want to get some idea of what the Milky Way looks like, go outdoors on a cloudless night at the end of summer and you will see a wide, white band of stars stretching like a road across the sky.

What makes us sneeze?

The inside of our nose is very sensitive, and quick to signal the brain if anything irritates it. So if we inhale something like pepper, which tickles or burns, the brain orders a sneeze to get rid of it. First of all we breathe in, quickly and deeply. Then, when the lungs are full of air, the windpipe closes. Next, the stomach muscles squeeze hard so that the air in the lungs is compressed. The windpipe opens — and the air rushes out through the nose to blow away whatever is causing the trouble.

27TH JUNE

Who is the Pope?

The Pope is the head of the Roman Catholic Church. St Peter was the first Pope. The present one, John Paul II, is 266th. The Pope is elected by the College of Cardinals, a group of Bishops who are responsible for governing the Catholic Church. He lives in the Vatican, in Rome.

What is soil?

Soil is the top layer of earth, covering the hard rocks beneath, from which plants can draw their food. It is made up of a mixture of mineral substances (sand, clay, chalk) and decayed animal and vegetable matter. The differences in soils are caused by the different mixtures of these things. Good growing soil always contains plenty of organic matter (matter which was once part of a living thing, a plant or animal). At certain times of the year farmers put manure or compost (rotted-down leaves and stems) on their fields to keep the soil rich and easy to work.

Because there are Roman Catholics all over the world, the Pope is a very powerful man. Recent Popes such as John XXIII who died in 1963, have used their influence in an effort to try and persuade the countries of the world to live at peace with each other.

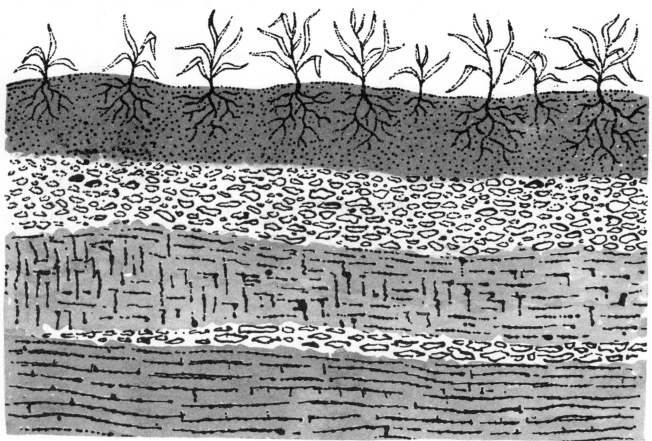

What is the Louvre?

The Louvre, in Paris, was once a palace of the French kings. Today there are no more kings of France, so it holds a splendid museum of art and antiques, which is recognised as one of the finest in the world. When Napoleon Bonaparte was master of most of Europe he filled the Louvre with art treasures looted from many countries. When he was defeated, most of these were given back, but the collections were built up again with paintings and statues obtained more honestly. In the Louvre you can see famous paintings and statues, like the Mona Lisa, the Venus de Milo, the Winged Victory of Samothrace, and many, many more.

Why do some insects shine?

Some insects produce a cold, chemical light. In most cases, such as those of the firefly and the glow worm, this light is produced to attract a mate. In others it is used to frighten away creatures which would otherwise eat the insect. The headlamp click beetle, for instance, which lives in the jungles of South America, has two great spots of light just behind its head. To any animal coming across the beetle at night, these spots look like enormous shining eyes — and the beetle is left alone.

What is the meaning of July?

Julius Caesar, the great Roman general, gave his name to July. Among the many things Caesar did was to re-arrange the Roman calendar. This gave him a problem with the name of the seventh month. In the old calendar it had been the fifth month, and this was the meaning of its name *Quintilis*. Caesar realised that it would be silly to have the seventh month with a name like 'The Fifth', so he decided to call it after himself — and Julius became July.

un-sticky thread in the middle where it waits for its prey. Though the webs look delicate, they are very strong. And though they look complicated, it takes a spider little time to make one — as your mother knows when she does the housework!

3RD JULY

How far is the earth from the sun?

2ND JULY

How does a spider spin a web?

A spider can produce a silky substance from tiny openings on its underside. To spin a web it starts by making a frame of this silk, attaching it to firm objects, such as twigs or brickwork. When the frame is finished, the spider fixes spokes of silk across it, just like the spokes of a wheel. Then it arranges the sticky spiral thread across these spokes, leaving a platform of

The average distance of the earth from the sun is 93 million miles. We say 'average' because the earth goes round the sun in an egg-shaped path, not in a true circle. So in January we are $91\frac{1}{2}$ million miles away, and in June we are $94\frac{1}{2}$ million miles away — though it does not seem that we are three million miles nearer as we shiver through the winter!

118

Why do Americans celebrate on this date?

The Fourth of July is American Independence Day, when Americans celebrate the gaining of their freedom from British rule. America — or at least the thirteen states which existed then — once belonged to Britain, and the colonists who settled there were mainly of British origin, many of them descended from the Pilgrim Fathers. These colonists objected to paying taxes to the government in London when they were not allowed to send members to Parliament.

In 1775 fighting broke out between the colonists and British troops. On July 4th, 1776, the states issued their Declaration of Independence. Fighting in the War of Independence carried on until October, 1781, when the British General Cornwallis surrendered to George Washington at Yorktown. The final peace treaty, however, was not signed until September, 1783.

Washington became the first President of the United States, and ever since then July 4th has been a holiday, with parades and firework displays, all over the U.S.A.

Do animals live as long as men?

Though humans come very high up on the list of long-lived animals, there are several wild creatures which live longer. The giant tortoises of the Galapagos Island, for instance, live to be more than 400 years old. Crocodiles can reach 300, and the larger snakes live for more than a century. Animals with a life-span similar to that of a human being are the elephant and the parrot, both reaching 60 or 70 years of age. Most of the other animals we are familar with have quite short lives: a dog or cat, for instance, is very old at 15; a horse at 25.

What is a periscope?

The Greek words which make up the word 'periscope' mean 'to see around' — and that is exactly what a periscope does. It is an arrangement of mirrors in a tube which enables the watcher to peer over obstructions without being seen himself. The best-known periscopes are those used in submarines. They enable the captain to see what is happening on the surface while the submarine itself is several feet underwater. You can make a periscope for yourself with two small mirrors and a long, narrow, cardboard box.

7TH JULY

Which city lies partly in Europe and partly in Asia?

Istanbul, the largest city in Turkey, and one of the oldest in the world, has a long and tumultuous history. It stands mainly on the European side of the Bosporus, the narrow strait which divides Europe from Asia, and has suburbs on the Asiatic side, so it controls the only entrance to the Black Sea. The main part stands on a triangular promontory, washed on the north by the famous stretch of water called the Golden Horn. Like Rome, it is built on seven hills.

Istanbul was once called Byzantium, then became Constantinople when the Roman Emperor Constantine made it the capital of his Eastern, or Byzantine, Empire in A.D. 330. From then until it was overrun by the Turks in 1453, Constantinople preserved the Greek and Roman culture which was being destroyed by barbarian invasions in Western Europe, thus forming a link between the ancient and modern civilisations.

Despite many earthquakes, much of the architecture of this period still stands. One of the most famous Byzantine buildings is the great church of St Sophia, rebuilt by the Emperor Justinian I between 527 and 565 on the site of an earlier church of Constantine. After the Turkish invasion it became a mosque, and in 1935 a museum.

Of what use is a snake's tongue?

The snake's forked tongue, continuously flickering in and out, frightens many people. They think it is poisonous. But the tongue is completely harmless, and is used by the snake to help it smell. By constantly flickering in and out, the tongue collects tiny particles from the air and carries them back into the mouth. In the roof of the mouth are two small holes which are sensitive to smell, and which pick up the particles from the tongue. A snake does not open its mouth to flick out its tongue: this is because the upper jaw has a notch which allows the tongue to move freely in and out.

Why does a camel have a hump?

The camel is a relative of the deer and the giraffe; there are two kinds: the dromedary and the Bactrian camel. The dromedary, the Arabian camel, has one hump. The Bactrian, the Asiatic, camel has two. These humps store food in the form of fat. Many people think that the humps store water, but the water is kept in stomach pouches. The humps and the stomach pouches mean that the camel need neither eat nor drink for three days, even in the driest deserts.

122

How can we taste?

We taste, first of all, through the taste-buds on our tongue. These are clusters of sensitive cells which can tell whether the thing we are eating is sweet, bitter, sour or salty. Our sense of smell also helps us to taste by picking up finer flavours which our tongue misses: this is why it helps to hold your nose if you have to take a dose of particularly nasty medicine.

11TH JULY

Which is the highest mountain?

The highest mountain in the world is Everest, a peak 8,848 metres high in the Himalayas, on the border between Nepal and Tibet. If the height in metres is difficult to imagine, think of a mountain five and a half *miles* high. It was named after Sir George Everest, the man who first put it on a map and who died in 1866. Several climbers lost their lives trying to reach its summit, and it was not until 1953 that the mountain was conquered by Sir Edmund Hillary and Sherpa Tensing, members of a British expedition led by Sir John Hunt.

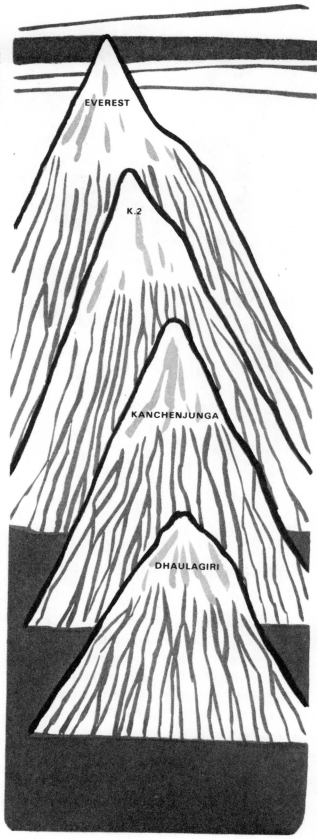

12TH JULY

13TH JULY

Which animals can change colour?

The chameleon, a lizard which lives in Africa and Madagascar, can change its colour to match its surroundings so that it is almost invisible to its prey and its enemies. This ability to change colour quickly is also given to the plaice. This flat fish, which lives on the bottom of the sea, changes its colour, and its pattern, to match the floor below it. Placed in an aquarium with a chessboard pattern of black and white squares on the bottom, it will turn itself into a copy of these squares.

Why does carbon dioxide gas put out fire?

A fire needs oxygen to burn, because fire itself is a combining of the oxygen in the air with the materials being burned. Carbon dioxide is of no use at all to a fire: in fact it is one of the waste gases formed by the fire itself. So if a fire is surrounded by carbon dioxide, and the oxygen cannot get through to it, it simply goes out.

That is why many fire extinguishers are filled with carbon dioxide.

124

Why do the French celebrate the Fall of the Bastille?

The Bastille, in Paris, was a strong fortress with eight towers which was used as a prison. So many people were imprisoned there simply for opposing the king that by 1789 it had come to stand for all that the people of France hated most. When the people rose against their king in the French Revolution, the Bastille was the first place to be attacked. On July 14th, 1789, it was captured. The prisoners were released, and the prison was razed to the ground. Since then, July 14th has been kept as a holiday in France.

15TH JULY

With what do we associate St Swithun's Day?

Swithun, or Swithin, was an English bishop and builder of many churches, who died in the year 862. Many people believe that if it rains on St Swithun's day, July 15th, it will rain for forty days. This is because when St Swithun's coffin was removed from Winchester Cathedral in 971, it was delayed for a long time by heavy rain.

125

What is copper?

Copper is a reddish-brown metal which is easily worked and which mixes well with other metals to form useful *alloys*. Mixed with tin it becomes bronze: mixed with zinc it becomes brass. It does not rust, as iron does, and is therefore very useful for making boilers, pipes and tanks for our household water systems. Our ancestors found out how to use copper, and how to turn it into bronze, about 2,000 years before Christ.

What are the continents?

The continents are the main divisions of the land on earth, and there are six of them: Africa, North America, South America, Asia, Australia and Europe. Some people argue that there should be five: that Europe and Asia should be lumped together to form Eurasia. Others argue that Antarctica should be called a continent, so making seven. You may come across the name Australasia: this includes Australia, New Zealand and all the nearby islands.

How did people first begin to write?

People learned to draw and paint long before they knew how to write, and writing grew out of pictures. Men discovered that they could leave messages for each other by drawing little pictures of the things they wanted to mention. After a while, they found that drawing complete pictures was tiresome, so they left bits out and produced simple signs for different objects.

A good example of this early picture language is the *hieroglyphs* of ancient Egypt. These hieroglyphs are still with us today, because the Egyptians carved and painted them on their great tombs and temples. From the Egyptian writing grew the alphabet of the Phoenicians. And from this came all the alphabets in use today, even though our own Roman alphabet looks so very different from, say, the Arabic alphabet.

The earliest of all written alphabets, though it died out during the Christian era, was the cuneiform or 'wedge-writing' of the Sumerians, who lived in what is now Iraq. Their writing consisted of wedge-shaped symbols made on soft clay by a pointed stick, and dates from 3,500 years before the birth of Christ.

127

What is the moon?

What is platinum?

Platinum is a rare and valuable metal, white in colour, and next to silver and gold the easiest to work. It is used a lot in the making of rings and jewellery but, because it has a great resistance to chemicals which would dissolve other metals away, it is also used a lot in chemical apparatus and in certain types of machinery.

The moon is the satellite of the earth, travelling round and round us just as the earth travels round the sun. It takes $29\frac{1}{2}$ days to go round us and, during that time, turns round once on itself. This means that it keeps the same side of its face towards us, and, until a Russian rocket photographed the far side in 1961, nobody had ever seen it.

As we discovered earlier, the moon is a dead world, with no air or water or life of any kind. Even its light is not its own: it is merely reflected sunlight. This is why the moon appears to change its shape at different times of the month: when the face lit by the sun is the one turned away from us, then we do not see it at all.

The moon is very small — its width is

only a quarter that of the earth. It travels round us at a distance of 221,000 miles at its nearest and 253,000 at its farthest.

When the American astronauts returned from their trip to the moon, they brought with them samples of rock and dust that they had collected from the moon's surface. Scientists have since examined these samples and have discovered facts about the moon which were previously unknown.

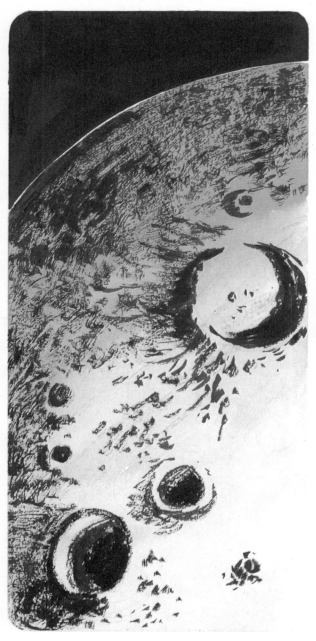

What are tides?

Though the force of gravity of the moon is weak, it is strong enough to be felt on earth. The pull of the moon causes the water in the earth's oceans to 'heap up' directly underneath it. As the earth turns, the moon holds this bulge of water steady so that eventually it reaches land and washes ashore as a tide.

This heaping up of water happens at the same time on the side of the earth facing away from the moon, and this is why we have two tides a day: there are two bulges of deep water going round the earth at the same time.

What is an echo?

An echo is caused by sound waves striking a solid object and bouncing back the way they came. This is why, in a valley or a cave, you can shout 'Hello!', and shortly after hear your own voice shouting 'Hello!' back to you. Echoes, interesting though they are, are often a problem to architects. A great deal of thought has to go into the building of a concert hall, to make sure the echo does not spoil the performance, or into the building of a factory, to make sure that the noise of the machinery is not magnified by echoes until it becomes unbearable.

Where did the goldfish originate?

The goldfish is a member of the carp family and is found in its wild state in China and Japan. In the wild, however, it is a dull green in colour and not very pretty.

The Chinese discovered that some of the fish had gold patches on their skin, and, by breeding from eggs laid by these fish, soon had fish which were gold all over. Then both the Chinese and the Japanese began to breed goldfish of many different shapes, choosing for parents those fish which had long fins, large eyes, or oddly-shaped bodies. They even produced a *black* goldfish.

Nowadays, of course, goldfish are kept and bred all over the world. You may have one yourself.

What are nursery rhymes?

We all remember the rhymes about Little Jack Horner, the Grand Old Duke of York, Old King Cole, and so on. These are rhymes which for generations have been passed on from parents to children. Most of these rhymes, however, were not made up for children: they referred to real people and real happenings, and generally poked fun at them. The Grand Old Duke of York, for instance, was a general who made rather a mess of things. You will see now how the rhyme poked fun at him:

The Grand Old Duke of York,
He had ten thousand men,
He marched them up to the top of the hill
And he marched them down again.

And when they were up they were up,
And when they were down they were down.
But when they were only half way up
They were neither up nor down.

What is coal?

Many millions of years ago, much of the world was covered by warm swamps, in which grew many kinds of giant trees and ferns. As these plants died, they rotted down to form great layers of peat. These layers became covered with mud or sand and sank further down, being pressed tighter and tighter, until they turned into the soft, shiny rock we know as coal. Now and again, in the coal you burn in your grate at home, you may come across the impression of a leaf, or the fossil shell of a large water snail. These were alive all those years ago, and in dying sank into the swamp to be turned into coal along with everything else.

very destructive. Though seldom more than a quarter of a mile across, and seldom lasting more than an hour, it moves in a straight line at speeds of up to 40 miles an hour, uprooting trees and wrecking buildings with whirling winds which at its centre can reach 200 miles an hour.

A hurricane is bigger and more widespread and any wind over 75 miles an hour is given the name. True hurricanes, however, are the tropical cyclones which occur over the West Indies and in the Gulf of Mexico, hitting the islands and mainland with great force and doing widespread damage. From August to October each year several hurricanes hit the American coast; these are given names like 'Betsy' so that people can follow their movements on radio and TV.

What is the difference between a tornado and a hurricane?

Tornadoes and hurricanes both belong to the spiral wind systems known as cyclones.

A tornado is a very small and fierce whirlwind, which at sea causes water-spouts by whipping up the water and carrying it many metres up into the air. On land it is

Who were the Vikings?

For nearly three hundred years, from the end of the eighth century to the middle of the eleventh, Europe and the Mediterranean were terrorised by Vikings, fierce warrior-farmers from Scandinavia, who put to sea in their longships to seek more wealth than the soil of their own countries would yield.

The Vikings, or Norsemen, came from Norway, Sweden, and Denmark, and seemed to be unbeatable on land or sea. During the first years of the Viking raids — they began by burning the British monastery at Lindisfarne in 793 — all they wanted was plunder. But later they began to settle and farm the land which their swords had won for them.

To the west, they colonised parts of England, Scotland, Ireland, France, Greenland — and, as you have read, even reached America. To the south they ravaged the coasts of Spain, Italy and North Africa. To the east they moved far into Russia, Turkey and even Persia.

They occupied much of central and northern England — in Alfred the Great's time the area was called the 'Danelaw' — and if you come from these areas you may have some Viking blood in your veins.

How does a compass work?

A compass tells us which way is north, south, east or west, and is of great help to sailors, airmen and explorers. It works very simply. When a needle or thin piece of steel is magnetised and balanced exactly in the middle, one end points to the north and the other to the south. No matter how much it is swung round, it always returns to this position. So the magnetised needle is placed on a dial, on which are marked all the points of the compass. To find out which way you are going, you let the needle point to north, then turn the dial so that the north marked on it points the same way. The other marks on the dial now point exactly to east, west, south and so on.

28TH JULY

What is a fossil?

A fossil is the stony remains of an animal or plant which has been buried in the earth for many thousands of years. When an animal dies in water or swampy ground, its body sinks down and is covered over with mud. In time this mud hardens into rock, leaving a cast of the animal's skeleton. Even if this skeleton has been dissolved away, by the time we dig up the rock, we have a perfect replica of it in the cast. Other fossils are made by the bones of the animal, or the stems and leaves of the plant, being replaced by minerals which turn into stone. So we find skeletons and even trees made out of stone! You can see many fine specimens of fossils in the Natural History Museum in London, and your own town museum will have some local examples.

and rail causeway, but there are no roads or railways in the city, just a hundred and seventy canals. The only way to travel is by boat, or on foot. One of the most famous sights of Venice is the gondolas, long, black, flat-bottomed boats, steered by cheerfully dressed 'gondoliers'. By the fourteenth century, Venice was the strongest sea-power in Europe, and became very wealthy. As a result, the city is full of richly decorated churches and palaces, and is very beautiful.

31ST JULY

What is pepper?

The pepper we sprinkle on our food is made from the dried berries of a climbing shrub, *Piper nigrum*. Black pepper is ground from the whole berries, white pepper from the seed after the outer husk has been removed.

There are also things called sweet peppers, which we find whole in certain pickles, and which can also be ground. These are the fruits of shrubs grown in South America.

30TH JULY

What is different about Venice?

Venice is built, not on solid ground, but on a hundred and twenty tiny mud islands just off the coast of Northern Italy. In the fifth century A.D., refugees from the mainland were driven on to these islands by barbarian invasions from the north. Wooden piles were driven into the mud, and buildings were built on top of these. Today, Venice is connected to the mainland by a long road

What is the meaning of August?

The Romans used to call August *Sextilis*, the sixth month. But when Julius Caesar reformed the calendar the name no longer suited it. Finally the Romans changed it to August to honour and flatter their Emperor Augustus, grand-nephew of the great Caesar.

Who was Charlemagne?

Charlemagne (the name means 'Charles the Great') was King of the Franks at the end of the eighth century. He was the strongest ruler in Europe, and soon his kingdom stretched from the borders of Spain, across France, Germany, Austria, Holland, Belgium, Switzerland, through Italy as far south as Rome, and even included parts of what are now Poland, Czechoslovakia, Hungary and Yugoslavia.

The most important of his campaigns, though, was when he went to Rome to rescue the Pope from the Lombards. Charles was very impressed by the fact this city, the centre of art and learning in Europe, and of the Christian Church, had no protector, and in A.D. 800, the Pope crowned him the first of the Holy Roman Emperors. Not only was Charlemagne a great Christian warrior, but he gave to his Empire good laws, a strong government, and good schools.

What is a volcano?

A volcano — named after Vulcan, the Roman god of fire — is a cone-shaped mountain built by molten rock and ash which pours from a crack in the surface of the earth. Volcanoes occur where the crust of the earth is thin or weakened by a fault. A volcano grows very quickly once the earth opens up — quite large ones are built up in a matter of months. Sometimes a volcano will lie dormant, or quiet, for many years. Occasionally a volcano will be 'plugged' by the molten rock, or lava, cooling and hardening in its crater. When the pressure again builds up inside, either the plug is blown out, the mountain cracks — or the whole thing explodes. Pompeii, in Italy, was destroyed by the explosion of Monte Somma in A.D. 79, and, in 1883, two-thirds of the East Indian island of Krakatoa was blown up by a volcano's explosion.

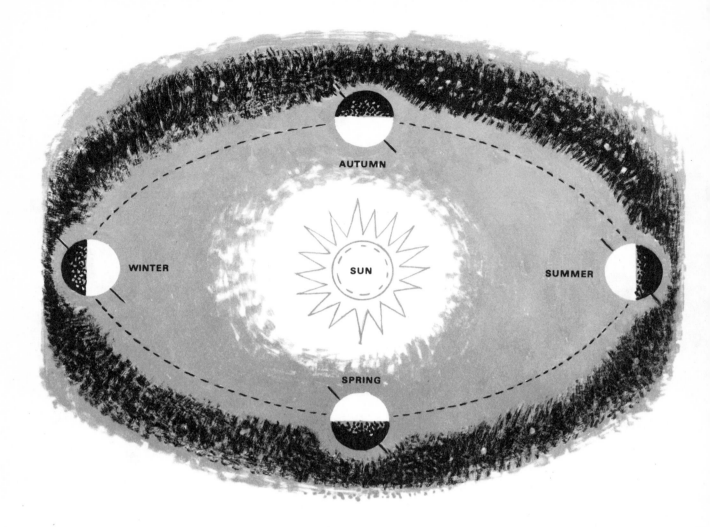

AUTUMN

WINTER

SUN

SUMMER

SPRING

What keeps the earth going round the sun?

If you have a ball on the end of a piece of string and whirl it round your head, the ball will swing round in a circle, keeping the string pulled tight. If the string were to break, the ball would stop going round in a circle and shoot away from you.

Imagine that the string is the pull of gravity exerted by the sun on the planets, and that the pull of the ball as it swings round is the 'centrifugal' force exerted by the earth, and it will help you to understand how the earth goes round the sun. In other words, the sun is pulling one way, the earth is pulling the other, and we circle round at the point where these two forces balance each other. If the sun suddenly lost its gravity, the earth would shoot off into space, propelled by the centrifugal force it has built up through millions of years of circling. It would be the same action as if the string had broken between you and the ball. On the other hand, if the earth were somehow to lose its centrifugal force, we should be drawn into the sun and burned up. Luckily for us there is no possibility of either of these things happening.

What is phosphorus?

Phosphorus is a chemical element which exists in nature mixed with other chemicals to form rock phosphate. It is extracted from the phosphate as white phosphorus, a curious, pale-yellow waxy substance which glows in the dark, is highly poisonous, and which can catch fire just by being exposed to the air. For this reason it is stored in water. White phosphorus can be changed, by heating it without air, into red phosphorus, which is not poisonous and can be kept safely in the open. Red phosphorus is used in the making of matches. Both kinds can be burned to form phosphorus oxide, which is used to make phosphoric acid. This acid is used for the manufacture of many things, from jellies to detergents, fertilisers and paints.

6TH AUGUST

How does a nettle sting?

The leaves and stems of a nettle are covered with hairs. Some of these are quite ordinary but others, longer than the rest, are stinging hairs. These are hollow and have at the bottom a little gland which holds a drop of formic acid. The ends of the hairs are sharp and brittle: they pierce the skin of a human or small animal, and then break off, allowing the acid to squirt through the hole in the skin and cause the sting. The old saying,

Very gently stroke a nettle
And it will sting you for your pains.
But grasp it like a man of mettle
And it as soft as silk remains,

is a true one. If you grasp a nettle firmly, the hair breaks off near the base and the sharp tips are unable to pierce the skin.

Are seashells alive?

The empty shells you find washed up by the tide, are of course, not alive. But they once protected a soft, flabby creature called a *mollusc*. There are many different kinds of molluscs in the sea — oysters, whelks, winkles, and barnacles — and they live in the armour they have grown themselves. If you look around the rocks, or on the piles of a pier, after the tide has gone down, you will find creatures like the barnacle, mussel and limpet, locked tight in their shells, waiting for the water to return. The mollusc family is a large one, and includes our garden snails and slugs (though the slug's shell is tiny and soft), and the giant squids which live in the ocean depths.

Why was the Colosseum built?

The Colosseum, the ruins of which still stand proudly in Rome, was built in the first century after Christ by the Emperors Vespasian and Titus. It is a large amphitheatre, rather like our football stadiums but much grander, and was built mainly by Jewish prisoners captured by the Romans in the battle for Jerusalem. Beautiful though it is, the Colosseum was the scene of some dreadful happenings. Its purpose was, like our football grounds, to provide entertainment for the people of Rome. But their idea of entertainment was very different: inside the Colosseum fights to the death took place between gladiators, or between wild beasts and Christian prisoners.

Where does the moon go to in the daytime?

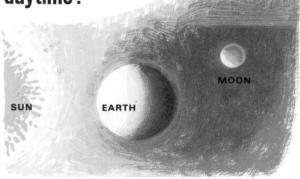

Seldom, during the day, can we see the moon. Sometimes it is for the simple reason that it is on the other side of the earth from us, and we have to wait until night falls for it to appear. At other times it is in the sky above us, but is invisible because the sun is shining so brightly that our eyes cannot pick out its pale glow. In the early morning or evening, the sun and moon can sometimes be seen in the sky. At these times the sun is not shining so brightly as to dazzle us, and we can see the moon quite clearly.

10TH AUGUST

What is an evergreen tree?

Most of our trees in Britain are deciduous, that is, their leaves fall every autumn and new ones grow the following spring. Certain trees, however, like the holly and the conifers (cone-bearing trees like the fir, the Norway spruce, and the pine) are evergreen. The name really explains itself: the trees stay green all winter through because the leaves stay on. The leaves or needles of the holly stay on the branches for about four years before falling off and letting others take their place. Because the leaves of an evergreen have to stand up to severe weather such as snow and wind storms, and last so much longer, they are smaller and thicker-skinned than those of the deciduous trees.

What is quicksilver?

Quicksilver, or mercury, is a heavy silver-coloured metal which is liquid in ordinary temperatures. If a blob of mercury is dropped on to a flat surface, it breaks into many smaller blobs which roll away very swiftly — hence the name quicksilver. Mercury comes from an ore called cinnabar, or vermilion, which is mined mainly in Spain. It is used, among other things, for coating the backs of mirrors to make them reflect, and in thermometers and barometers. Be very careful if you ever get hold of any mercury: it is highly poisonous.

CINNABAR
(SULPHIDE OF MERCURY)

What was the Inquisition?

The Inquisition began as a tribunal set up by Pope Gregory IX in 1233 to seek out people who had religious views different from those of the Roman Catholic Church at the time, who were called 'heretics', and to get them to change their ideas. From this beginning it soon turned into a terrible thing which lasted for hundreds of years, and in which many thousands of people who refused to change their ideas were tortured and burned alive. The Inquisition spread through Europe — its methods were used even in England under Mary Tudor — and to the Spanish colonies in South America. The Spanish Inquisition, begun in 1481, was worse than the one in Rome. The first Grand Inquisitor — Torquemada — was said to have had two thousand people burned alive.

What is an orchestra?

An orchestra is a large number of musicians, with instruments of different kinds, who together make the rich and beautiful sounds we enjoy so much. A modern symphony orchestra can be made up of a hundred or more players. Familiar as it is to us, however, the orchestra did not take shape until the second half of the eighteenth century. Before that there were groups of musicians who played together with varying kinds of success, but it was not until Haydn, Mozart and others worked to get the kind of sound they wanted that the modern orchestra emerged, based on the three families of instruments: strings, woodwind and brass.

13TH AUGUST

Which bird lays the largest egg?

The ostrich is the largest living bird. And it also lays the largest egg, white in colour and weighing 1.4 kilograms. The eggs are laid in an open nest on the ground and are guarded by the male during the night and the female during the day.

Why does bread go mouldy if it is left?

Mould is a fungus, one of the great family of primitive plants which includes the mushroom and toadstool. And the air we breathe is full of the spores, or seeds, of many different kinds of these fungi. The spores eventually land and, if they find food and water — their favourites are decaying animal or vegetable matter — they begin to grow. Bread is an excellent landing-ground for mould-spores: it is full of little holes, which mean the spores can find safe anchorage, it is damp and full of nourishment.

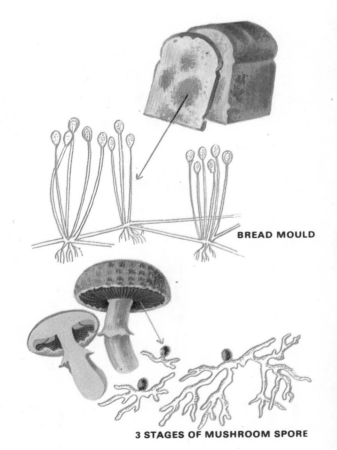

BREAD MOULD

3 STAGES OF MUSHROOM SPORE

What is the Eiffel Tower?

The Eiffel Tower, rising 300 metres over the centre of Paris, was built for the great Paris Exhibition of 1889 by Alexandre Eiffel, a brilliant engineer who, among other great works, also designed the framework for the Statue of Liberty in New York harbour. Some of you may have been lucky enough to go to Paris and see the Tower for yourself: others may see the English imitation of it, the 158-metre-high Blackpool Tower.

Where are the stars in the day-time?

What is a kiwi?

The kiwi, found only in New Zealand and adopted by that country as its emblem, is one of the world's strangest and least bird-like of all birds. Unable to fly, having only the tiniest of wings, and covered by feathers that look more like hair, it appears only at night. It carries its nostrils at the end of its 15-centimetre long slender bill, and by smell it sniffs out the earthworms under the forest soil. Kiwis live in long burrows under the earth near tree roots.

In the daytime the stars are where they have always been — up there in the sky above us. Like the moon, the stars cannot be seen during the day because the sun's light is much brighter than theirs and our eyes cannot pick them out. It is interesting to watch the sky in the early evening and see which stars appear first as the sunlight fades. You will find that those you spot early on still shine the brightest when all the others have come out.

145

What is a ballot?

A ballot is a system of secret voting. It is done in elections for Parliament, or for local councils, by putting a cross on a piece of paper against the name of the man, or woman, of your choice. The paper is then folded and slipped into a box with the votes of everybody else, so that when the votes are finally counted, nobody can tell who has voted for any particular party. The word 'ballot' comes from the French *ballotte*, or 'little ball'. This comes from the system of using small balls of different colours to signify agreement or disagreement over, say, the election of a man to membership of a club. You may hear that a man has been 'blackballed' on applying for club membership. This means that someone has voted against him by dropping in a black ball.

What is the difference between a toad and a frog?

First, let us look at the similarities between a toad and a frog: they are both amphibians — that is, they spend their lives partly in the water and partly on the land — and are related; they both lay eggs in the water which hatch into tadpoles; they both have webbed feet and bodies of roughly the same shape; they both eat roughly the same food — worms, insects and slugs. Now the differences: toads spend more time away from the water, their skin is duller, rougher and drier, their limbs are shorter and they cannot jump so far as the frog. Frogs' eggs,

Is an ass related to a horse?

Horses, asses and zebras spring from a common ancestor, and the horse and the ass are still related closely enough to be able to breed. With a horse as the mother and an ass as the father, the offspring is a mule. A mule is as strong as a horse, but as small and agile as an ass, so it is used as a carrying animal in rough country. The mule is a very stubborn animal But the curious thing is this — the mule itself is unable to have children. This means that the two animals have become different enough for the two strains of blood not to be able to mix permanently again.

or spawn, are laid in a jelly-like mass; toads' eggs are laid in strings and wound around the stems of water plants. Toad tadpoles are smaller and darker than those of frogs. Though toads are ugly, they do not have the nasty habits some people think they have: they do not have a poisonous bite (in fact they are toothless), and they do not give you warts. Mind you, if you handle a toad, it does leave a rather unpleasant smell on your hands: it has a special fluid in the wart-like knobs on its skin which it uses as a defence against other animals — like you!

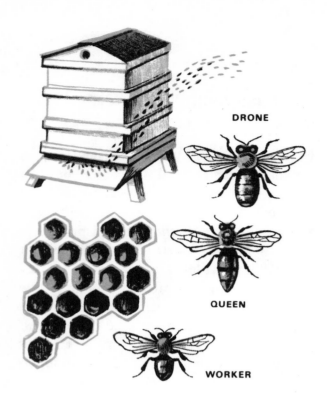

DRONE

QUEEN

WORKER

Why is Salzburg so famous?

Salzburg is an ancient and beautiful city in north-west Austria, famous as the birthplace of Mozart and for its yearly music festival.

Wolfgang Amadeus Mozart was born in 1756, the son of a violinist employed by the Archbishop of Salzburg. Both Wolfgang and his older sister were brilliant musicians from an early age, and, from the time Wolfgang was six, their father used to take them on tours to play to kings and queens all over Europe. Then, in his teens, Mozart became even more famous as a composer, especially after he met, and was inspired by, Haydn. He wrote all kinds of music: religious and choral, chamber and orchestral, and opera. His most famous operas include *The Marriage of Figaro*, *The Magic Flute*, and *Don Giovanni*.

Mozart died, exhausted and poverty-stricken, at the age of only thirty-five.

22ND AUGUST

Why do bees live in hives?

Bees, like ants, are social animals: that is, they live together in great colonies, each with its own job to do to help the colony as a whole to survive. Man discovered very early that it was easier to collect honey from bees if he gave them a home, instead of letting them build their own nest in the wild. These homes, or hives, used to be made out of straw, but nowadays they are built of wood. Inside there are frames on which the bees can build their honeycombs. When the frames are full of honey they are lifted out and empty ones put in their place. In reward for the honey, the bees get a warm, dry home, and during the winter are fed on syrup by the beekeeper.

What are bones made of?

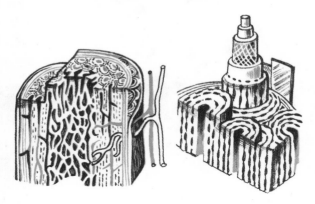

The hard part of a bone is made by the body from calcium. This is why it is important that growing children should eat foods rich in calcium, like milk, eggs and cheese. The outer part of the bone is solid and hard. The inside contains a spongy layer of bone around a hollow core. Inside this spongy layer are blood vessels, cells, nerves and water. The hollow space down the middle of the bone is filled with marrow, a very important tissue which makes the red blood corpuscles and certain kinds of white ones.

Who was Simon Bolivar?

As the leader of rebel armies against the Spaniards, Simon Bolivar won independence for six South American states. Bolivia is named after him.

Bolivar was born in Venezuela in 1783. During a visit to Europe as a young man, he was very impressed by Napoleon's battles against the old established rulers, and vowed to liberate his own country from the Spanish Empire. He joined rebel troops in Venezuela in 1810, while Spain was involved in the Napoleonic Wars, but when the rebels were defeated, had to flee to New Granada (now Colombia). He had to flee again from Colombia, but returned to defeat the Spaniards in 1819, and was made President and military dictator. In 1821, he liberated his homeland, Venezuela, and Ecuador. In 1824, he had won most of Peru, and there was only one small area in South America still ruled by the Spaniards. This was freed in 1826, and the people chose to call it Bolivia.

Bolivar was disappointed with the results of his work. The new South American states gradually withdrew from the union he had tried to form, and he retired from their affairs of government in the year 1830 and died soon afterwards.

Which is the world's smallest bird?

There are five hundred different kinds of humming-bird living in the forests of South and Central America. Some of them are as big as the birds we see in our gardens, but most of them are very tiny indeed: the smallest, without their feathers, are little larger than a bee: these tiny, darting, brilliant creatures build nests the size of a walnut shell and lay eggs the size of a small pea.

How does a magnet work?

A magnet is a substance — generally metallic — which has the power of attracting iron, steel, nickel and certain other substances. It has this power because it is charged with a kind of electrical energy. In a straight bar magnet the power of attraction is contained in the two ends, or poles. These poles, north and south, attract each other. If you place the north pole of one magnet against the south pole of another, they will cling together. However, if you put two north, or two south poles together, they will push each other away.

You can see a magnet's 'lines of force' by placing a bar magnet under a piece of paper and sprinkling the paper with iron filings. The filings will arrange themselves on the paper in the pattern made by the 'force-field.'

If you tie a piece of thread to the centre

of a bar magnet and let it hang, it will swing round until the north pole points north, and the south pole points south: it is then acting as a compass, following the line of the magnetic field of the earth.

The name 'magnet' comes from Magnesia, in Greece, where the first natural magnets, or lodestones, which were pieces of magnetic iron ore, were found.

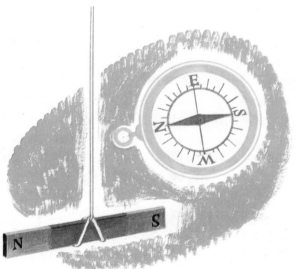

Why is Versailles so famous?

Versailles is a town ten miles outside Paris. But when people speak of Versailles, they generally mean the great palace, built by King Louis XIV in the late seventeenth century as the home for the French royal family. While the French monarchy existed, up to the time of the Revolution, in 1789, it was the scene of many glittering occasions.

Since then, many other important things have happened in its richly-furnished rooms. In 1783, the Treaty of Versailles ended the American War of Independence. And in 1919 another treaty, with the same name, officially ended the First World War between Germany and the Allies. This treaty was intended to solve the problems which caused the war, and among its conditions was the setting up of the League of Nations, the forerunner of the United Nations. Many Germans regarded the treaty as unjust, and it was one of the causes of World War II.

What is atomic energy?

At one time it was thought that the atom was the smallest piece of matter it was possible to have, and that it was impossible to divide it or to change it. However, it was discovered that it was possible to split an atom, so releasing the energy which held the nucleus, or centre core, together. This process is known as *fission*.

The release of energy causes the explosion of an atom bomb. But the same process can be controlled in the reactor of an atomic power station and the energy, given off in the form of heat, used to produce steam for turning generators which make electricity.

Another kind of atomic energy is that known as *fusion*. What happens here is that the nuclei of two atoms join together to make a new, single nucleus. This nucleus

is smaller than the original two put together, and needs less energy to bind it. The spare energy released by fusion rushes out to cause an explosion, and this is the energy used in the hydrogen bomb. Unlike fission, however, fusion cannot be controlled, and its only use so far is in destruction.

What were the Seven Wonders of the World?

The Seven Wonders of the ancient world were the Pyramids of Egypt, the Hanging Gardens of Babylon, the Colossus of Rhodes, the Temple of Diana at Ephesus, the Statue of Jupiter at Athens, the Tomb of Mausolus and the Lighthouse of Alexandria. Of these only the Pyramids survive today.

The largest of the Pyramids, the great Pyramid of Cheops, took a hundred thousand slaves twenty years to build. And it was built, 6,600 years ago, solely to provide Cheops with a tomb!

The Hanging Gardens of Babylon were built by King Nebuchadnezzar inside his palace grounds. One and a half hectares of gardens were laid out in terraces which stood on arches twenty three metres high.

The Colossus of Rhodes was a gigantic bronze statue of Helios, the sun god, which stood at the entrance of the harbour on the island of Rhodes, looking out over the Aegean sea. Finished in 260 B.C., it took the sculptor, Chares, twelve years to build. After standing for sixty years it was wrecked by an earthquake, and lay in pieces for centuries until the Saracens sold it for scrap.

The Temple of Diana, at Ephesus in what

PYRAMIDS

HANGING GARDENS OF BABYLON

TEMPLE OF DIANA AT EPHESUS

JUPITER

COLOSSUS OF RHODES

TOMB OF MAUSOLUS

LIGHTHOUSE ON PHAROS

is now Turkey, contained a statue of the goddess Diana which was supposed to have fallen from heaven. It was destroyed, along with the city, by the Goths in A.D 262.

We know what the statue of Jupiter looked like because it appeared on ancient Greek coins, but today there is no trace of it. With a body said to have been carved in ivory, and wearing a robe made of gold, the statue was made for the temple at Olympia by the great sculptor Phidias, who died in 432 B.C.

The tomb of King Mausolus (from which we get our word mausoleum) was built by his widow at Halicarnassus, a Greek city in Asia Minor (which is now Turkey), in the fourth century B.C. It stood over forty two metres high and was topped by great statues of Mausolus and his Queen, Artemisia. Some of the smaller statues from it are in the British Museum.

The Lighthouse of Alexandria, in Egypt, stood at the entrance to the harbour on the island of Pharos. From its location the Greeks borrowed the word *pharos* to mean lighthouse. Built of white stone by Ptolemy the First in the third century B.C., it soared 122 metres above the harbour.

ROME

SPAIN

Which country has an eagle as its national emblem?

GERMANY

Several countries have the eagle as their national emblem, among them Spain, Germany, Albania and Austria.

These European eagles are descended from the eagle of the standard of the Roman Empire, which was adopted by Charlemagne as the badge of his empire. The United States of America has the eagle as its emblem, too, though why it was chosen is not quite clear, except that the Bald Eagle is common in the United States.

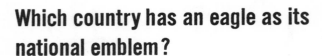

ALBANIA

U.S.A.

AUSTRIA

154

What is the meaning of September?

September was the seventh month of the old calendar, and when it became the ninth the Romans did not bother to rename it. Its name comes from *septem,* meaning seven.

Why is a centipede so called?

The many-legged creature you can see if you lift a stone in the garden gets its name from the Latin words *centum,* hundred, and *pes,* foot. However, it does not have anything like a hundred feet. The bodies of the different kinds of centipede are divided in segments, between fifteen and twenty-four of them, and each of these segments carries a pair of legs. A relation of the centipede is the millipede, whose name means 'thousand-foot', but there again it has not nearly so many. The centipede does much good in the garden by eating harmful insects. British centipedes cannot harm human beings, but some large tropical members of the family have very dangerous stings.

How does television work?

Television is one of those things we take for granted, but the process by which an event happening many miles away can be seen at the same time in your living room is one of man's great scientific achievements.

You have read how, with an ordinary camera, rays of light hit a piece of film and impress the picture upon it. In a television camera, the rays of light act in the same way, but fall instead on a collection of photo-electric cells which transform the light into electrical impulses. Strong light is turned into a strong current, weak light into a weak current. This current is then transmitted from the television studio to your set at home

The problem now is how to turn these electric impulses back into a picture. This is done inside the cathode ray tube of your set. At the back of the tube is a gadget called

an electron gun, which shoots out the current as an electron beam, on to the back of your screen. The back of the screen is coated with a fluorescent material which lights up when hit by the beam. The gun is 'aimed' by a scanning device which makes the thin line of the beam cross your screen very rapidly from left to right, drop slightly, cross again, drop again, and so on to the bottom — in very much the same way as your eyes scan the lines of a book. When the beam gets to the bottom it starts again at the top. Now comes a curious thing. The beam lights up the screen at only one point at a time. A television picture photographed by a very fast camera would show only one dot of light, and not a whole picture. What helps here is the fact that the human eye 'holds' an impression for a twelfth of a second after it has seen it. If the electron beam scanned the screen in less than a twelfth of a second, your eye would 're-member' the whole picture it had built up. In fact, the beam covers the whole of the screen, from top to bottom, twenty-five times a second — so, as far as your eyes are concerned, they are seeing a very clear and complete picture.

4TH SEPTEMBER

What is the House of Commons?

The House of Commons is one of the two Houses of Parliament which govern the United Kingdom and make its laws. The other is the House of Lords. Unlike the Lords, whose members are there simply because they belong to the peerage, members of the House of Commons are elected. Everyone in the country over the age of eighteen, with a few exceptions, can vote for the candidate of their choice at election times. A general election — that is an election in which all the seats in the House are voted for — must be held every five years. There are 630 members of the House of Commons: 511 for England, 71 for Scotland, 36 for Wales and 12 for Northern Ireland. Both Houses of Parliament meet in the Palace of Westminster though, of course, they each have their own chamber. The Commons are more powerful than the Lords, who survive mainly as a safeguard against silly or dangerous laws being put into effect.

Are birds warm-blooded?

Birds, though they are descended from cold-blooded reptiles and keep many reptilian features — like scaly legs, the laying of eggs and a horny mouth — are warm-blooded. Their body temperature, in fact, is higher than that of a human being. They live at a much faster rate than we do, eating more food for their size and using a great deal of energy in flying. Because of this, their hearts beat much more quickly and pump the blood round much faster. The birds' feathers, which keep a layer of warm air trapped all around the skin, keep in the body heat and so prevent energy being wasted in an attempt to keep warm.

Is an adder dangerous?

The adder, Britain's only poisonous snake, has a nasty bite which can kill children, old people, or people with bad hearts, if they are not treated in time. To a healthy adult its bite is not fatal, but is still very painful and frightening. Like most wild animals, however, the adder is mainly concerned with getting out of the way when alarmed, and only bites when trodden on, or when it sees no other way out of danger. So if you come across a snake, whether you recognise it as an adder or not, the best thing to do is not to try and catch it or kill it, but to let it glide swiftly away to safety.

What is the Dead Sea?

The Dead Sea is a large saltwater lake, forty-six miles long in Jordan. It lies 393 metres below sea level and is so salty that fish are unable to live in it — hence its name. It is mentioned often in the Bible by various names: the Salt Sea, the Sea of the Plain and the East Sea. The Arabic name for it is the Sea of Lot, and it was by its shores that Lot's wife was supposed to have been turned into a pillar of salt after the destruction of Sodom. The salt in the water makes the Dead Sea very easy to float in: it is even possible to lie full length in the water and read a newspaper.

8TH SEPTEMBER

Who was the 'Sun King'?

Louis XIV came to the throne of France in 1643, aged four years and eight months. His reign ended seventy-two years later in September 1st, 1715, four days before his seventy-seventh birthday. Not only was this reign the longest of any European monarch: it was also one of the most glorious periods in the whole history of France.

Louis did not really start to rule until 1660. In the same year he married Maria Theresa, a Spanish princess. Then he set out to make France the greatest power in Europe, and by 1678 he had built up quite a large empire. After that, however, his luck changed and France's army — which people had thought was unbeatable — suffered some big defeats, especially from William of Orange and his famous general, the Duke of Marlborough.

However, Louis was more than just a military-minded dictator. He encouraged music and the arts, and built the splendid palace of Versailles. So rich and glorious was his reign that he was given the nickname of the 'Sun King'.

Who was 'Buffalo Bill'?

William Frederick Cody, born in 1845, served as a scout with the United States Army in the old wild West. When the Kansas Pacific Railway was being built, Cody turned buffalo hunter to keep the workmen supplied with fresh meat, and this is how he got his name. He took part in many expeditions against the Indians, and became famous. In 1883 he founded his Wild West Show, which toured Europe. He died in 1917.

What is a cell?

A cell is the smallest piece of living matter: there is a lowly animal called an *amoeba* which is just one solitary cell: we ourselves are made up of countless millions of cells. The cell is called the 'building brick' of all plants and animals.

Each cell is made up of a central core called a *nucleus* and an outer part called the *cytoplasm,* in which food for the cell is stored. In a complicated animal, such as we are, different cells have different jobs to do and so vary in appearance, shape and colour, but all are basically made in the same way.

Who discovered penicillin?

Penicillin is a substance produced by certain fungi, or moulds. It was discovered in 1929 by the Scottish scientist Sir Alexander Fleming. He noticed that a dish, in which he had been growing some germs, had been 'invaded' by mould, and that around the mould the germs had been killed. During World War II the British and Americans helped each other to find out more about penicillin and its use as a germ-killer became widespread. Today it is one of the doctor's chief weapons in the fight against disease.

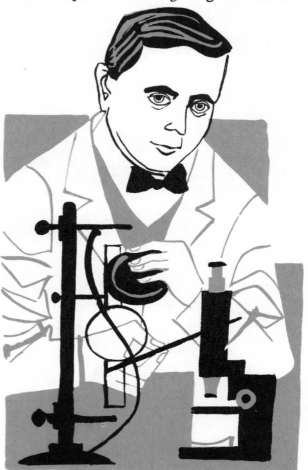

11TH SEPTEMBER

What is peat?

Peat is the remains of long-dead plants, compressed into a spongy, fibrous mass. It is part of a process similar to that by which plants eventually turn into coal, though peat bogs were laid down much later than the coal measures. Most British peat is made up of mosses. There is a lot in Ireland, where it is used as fuel.

Who was Don Quixote?

Spain's most famous author is Miguel de Cervantes, a novelist, playwright and poet who lived from 1547 to 1616. Though he wrote many works, he is best remembered for *Don Quixote,* the story of a mad knight who goes off in search of fame and adventure. In company with Sancho Panza his little, fat squire, Don Quixote does have many adventures — but none of them quite what he intended. This does not perturb him greatly, because he lives in a dream-world full of giants and damsels in distress. The best-known incident is that where Don Quixote attacks a group of windmills, thinking that they are giants. When his lance is smashed by the revolving sails, and he and his horse are sent rolling on the ground, Don Quixote still refuses to see the truth: he decides that the giants have been turned into windmills by a wicked wizard. The mounts of Quixote and his squire play a big part in the story. Quixote rides an ancient, skin-and-bones horse called Rosinante, and Panza rides an ass.

Why do some animals sleep all the winter?

The habit of some animals of sleeping through the winter months is called hibernation. Reptiles in cold countries hibernate because cold weather makes them so sluggish that it would be hard for them to stay awake even if they wanted to. Because their body is the same temperature as the air around them, they would quickly freeze to death if they stayed out in the open. Warm-blooded animals like the dormouse, the squirrel, the hedgehog and the bear, sleep because they would have difficulty in finding food during the months of ice and snow. Before they go to sleep they spend a lot of time eating so that they get nice and fat. During the long sleep they live off this fat, which their bodies have stored away. The squirrel hides nuts in secret places so that, if he should wake up on a warm winter day, he has food to eat. Should you find a hibernating animal, do not wake it: it would probably die.

What is granite?

Granite is a very hard rock, formed by fierce volcanic heat. It is much prized for building because of its great strength. Generally grey in colour, it can also be found in pink, red, green and yellow. In Britain, the finest granites come from Peterhead and Aberdeen, in Scotland, and from Cornwall.

Who was St Christopher?

You may have seen, fixed to the dashboard of a motor car, a medallion which shows a large man carrying the Christ-child over a river. This man is St Christopher, the patron saint of travellers. An old legend tells how Christopher, whose name then was Offero, set out to find the greatest king on earth and to serve him. He found a king and served him until he discovered that the king was afraid of the Evil One. So then he set off to find the Devil himself, thinking that he must be even braver.

He found the Devil and served him, until he saw the Devil shrink from a wooden cross. The Devil told Offero how he feared the man called Christ.

Offero again left and came to a hermit. The hermit told him the story of Christ, and also said that Christ did not want people to fight for Him, but to fight against evil by their example. Offero, however, said he was a very strong man and that he wanted to use his strength to help Christ. So the hermit took him to the banks of a swift and wide river, told him to live there and help other people by carrying them across. This Offero did, gladly.

One stormy night, a child appeared and asked to be taken across. Offero lifted him on to his shoulder and began the crossing. As he waded, the child became heavier and heavier, and it was all Offero could do to stagger to the opposite bank. And then the child told the strong man: 'I am Christ. I seemed heavy because I carry the sins and sorrows of the world. Because you have been kind to the weak, and carried Me on your shoulders, I will call you Christopher.'

This child vanished, leaving Christopher by the river bank. Henceforth, St Chrisropher became the patron saint of all those who set out on a journey.

Where do some birds go in the winter?

In the winter time a great many birds fly away from Britain to seek food and warmth in other countries. Their journeys are long and dangerous, and even the tiniest of birds undertake journeys of many hundreds of miles, some of it across the open sea. The wheatear, for instance, flies five thousand miles into the heart of Africa — and some of them have already travelled 2,500 miles from Greenland to England before they start this long second leg. The swallow and the swift fly right down to the tip of South Africa. The reed warbler and the lesser whitethroat fly to East Africa. Other birds make journeys which are shorter, but still dangerous for such tiny creatures: blackcaps and chiffchaffs, and some pied wagtails and song thrushes, fly to southern France, Spain and North Africa. What makes it even more amazing is that these journeys are undertaken again in the spring when the birds return to Britain.

Who founded the Red Cross?

A young Swiss banker named Jean Henri Dunant was visiting Italy in 1859 during the Austro-Sardinian War. Dunant saw the Battle of Solferino, and next day he was horrified by the forty thousand Austrian and French casualties still lying on the ground. In 1862 he published a book, pleading for governments to set up an international organisation for treatment of the wounded. In 1863, delegates from sixteen countries met in Geneva, Switzerland. In 1864, twenty-six European countries agreed to the Geneva Convention on treatment of those wounded in war, whatever side they belonged to, by nurses and doctors wearing the distinctive sign of the Red Cross.

What do woodpeckers eat?

When a woodpecker hammers on the bark of a tree, he is not doing it just for fun. He pecks away at the rotting bits of bark or wood to uncover the insects hiding underneath. And these insects he eats, picking them out of crevices with his long, barbed tongue.

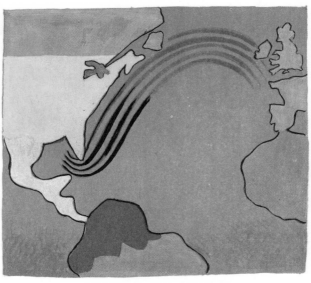

climate of Western Europe warmer than it ought to be, because the water coming from America has been warmed by its passage through the tropics. It helps the British climate, too: winds blowing across the Atlantic from North America make part of the Gulf Stream 'peel off' to form the North Atlantic Drift which flows around the British Isles.

What is the Gulf Stream?

The Gulf Stream is a great current of the North Atlantic Ocean which takes water from the coast of Africa, at the Equator, across to South America, up to North America and then back across the Atlantic to Western Europe, and down again to Africa. What it would look like, if you could see it all at once, would be a great clockwise swirl of water between Africa and the Americas. It is caused by the north-east trade winds, which blow the water across from Africa. The Gulf Stream makes the

Who were the Incas?

The Incas were the ancient rulers of Peru, and their name is also used to describe the people of the great empire which lasted for three hundred years until a Spanish expedition destroyed it.

A hundred and sixty-six men, led by Francisco Pizarro, conquered the Inca empire of twenty-four million people in 1533. They did it by capturing (and eventually killing) the Inca King, Atahualpa. The peasants were so used to being told what to do, and to having their lives ordered for them,

like those the Aztecs thought necessary.

Some of the Spaniards on the expedition, though they became rich men by the conquest, became sickened with what they had done: the civilisation they had destroyed was in many ways better than their own.

What is a wave?

When we look at waves on the sea, the water seems to be rolling forward. But really the water is only moving up and down, though the *movement* is travelling. If this is a little difficult to understand, think of the movement in a piece of rope when you take it by one end and flick it. The rope curves at the end nearest your hand and this curve travels to the far end — though the rope itself has not left your hand. A wave in the sea, like a sound wave in the air, is a *vibration*. Instead of travelling through the water, as sound travels through air, it travels on top of the water, making the surface rise and fall as it passes along.

that when their King was killed they simply became the slaves of the Spaniards.

Life in the empire, which covered roughly what is now Bolivia, Chile, Ecuador and Peru, was ordered from the cradle to the grave. Nobody was poor, nobody was rich (except for the small ruling class). Nobody went hungry. Under their rulers the peasants worked in the fields, built roads, irrigation systems and many fine buildings. Though Inca rule was firm, it was not cruel: there were no human sacrifices, for instance,

What were the Crusades?

The Crusades were expeditions undertaken by the Christian countries of Europe, between the eleventh and fourteenth centuries, to win back the Holy Land from the Mohammedans.

At first the Crusades were undertaken by the Christians in the spirit of real religious feeling, but later many men went to the Holy Land because of the prospect of loot and riches. There were also many quarrels between the Christian leaders, which helped the Mohammedans — mainly Turks and Arabs — to defeat them in battle. The First Crusade, asked for by Pope Urban II in 1095, was reasonably successful. The second Crusade, begun in 1144, failed because of quarrels. Our own King Richard I joined other rulers in the Third Crusade which ended in a truce with Saladin, of the Saracens, in 1191. The leaders of the Fourth Crusade in 1202 had forgotten all about the real purpose of the expedition. They did not even reach the Holy Land, but turned their armies against Constantinople to seize the wealth of the Byzantine Emperor. With this disgraceful episode the great Crusades died out, and only a few small ones were undertaken afterwards — including the ill-fated Children's Crusade about which you read earlier.

One good result of the Crusades was that some of the knowledge and learning of the East — including the Arabic numbers we use today — was brought back to Europe.

What is an amoeba?

An amoeba is a tiny animal which consists of just one cell. It belongs to the great family of microscopic animals called *Protozoa* and makes its home in the mud of ponds and streams. Looking like a little blob of jelly, the amoeba has no proper shape. When it wants to move anywhere it just flows. When it wants to eat, it just flows around its food, using as a stomach the space in which the food particle is trapped. When an amoeba becomes fully grown, it reproduces another amoeba. It does so very simply by just splitting in half. If you have a good microscope you could try looking for an amoeba in a drop of pond water. Some are big enough to be seen by the naked eye, but most are much smaller.

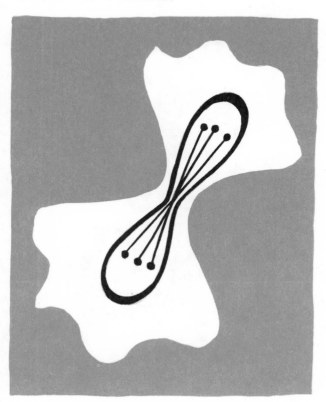

25TH SEPTEMBER

Where does oil come from?

It is strange to think that our civilisation which depends today so much on oil and petrol for transport, heat and power, is really being run on the decayed bodies of tiny sea creatures which died millions of years ago. As the creatures died, they were covered with layers of silt on the sea bed. Their bodies decayed, and the fatty parts turned into oil. Over the years the silt above them hardened into rock, and the oil was squeezed out of the harder layers and seeped through porous rocks like limestone or sandstone. Eventually, it reached another layer of hard rock, and there it was trapped, gradually filling up great hollows in the softer rock around it.

To reach the oil now we drill holes down to these hollows, and the oil shoots to the surface, forced up by the pressure of gas built up underground for millions of years.

What is the Koran?

Just as Christians have the Bible, so Mohammedans, or Moslems, have their holy book. This is the Koran, or Q'ran. Moslems believe that the Koran was told by God to their prophet Mohammed, and it contains several stories which are also in the Old Testament of the Bible.

27TH SEPTEMBER

What is the difference between an alligator and a crocodile?

It is not easy to tell the difference between an alligator and a crocodile — and if you were to meet one in the wild, you probably would not hang around long enough to make sure!

Alligators, however, are generally shorter than crocodiles. The Mississippi alligator grows to about 4.8 metres and the Chinese alligator to much less. The head is shorter and broader than the crocodile's. They are found, as the names suggest, respectively in North America and in parts of China.

Crocodiles are spread throughout Africa, Asia and Australia. Some of them grow very large indeed — monsters more than ten metres long have been killed.

There is a third member of the crocodile family — the cayman, of South America and the West Indies. The cayman, too, has a shorter, broader head than the crocodile and its nostrils have joined together to make one opening instead of two.

How does a barometer work?

There are two kinds of barometer: the mercury and the aneroid. Both measure the pressure of the air around us, and because of this they can be used to tell the height above sea level or to predict changes in the weather. They can measure height because the higher you go, the lower is the pressure of the air. And they can forecast changes in the weather because when the air pressure rises, it generally means the approach of dry or still weather: when it falls, it generally means the approach of wind, which brings with it rain and snow.

The mercury barometer consists of a long tube, closed at one end and curling round at the bottom into a cup shape. The tube is filled with mercury. When it is stood upright, some of the mercury runs from the tube into the cup, leaving an empty space at the top end of the tube. When the air pressure increases, it presses down on the cup of mercury and forces some of the mercury up the tube. When it falls, mercury from the tube runs into the cup. So we have the thin column of mercury in the tube rising and falling with the pressure. (You may have heard your father say: 'The glass is falling', after looking at the barometer, meaning that bad weather is on the way.) A mercury barometer is generally fitted with a mechanism which turns a pointer on a dial, so that changes can be easily read.

A more common kind of barometer in the home is the aneroid barometer. This consists of a round metal box, with no air inside it, attached to a spring mechanism which turns a pointer on a dial. When the air pressure is low, the spring pulls up the top

of the box, and turns the pointer to 'Rain'. When the air pressure increases, it pushes down the top of the box and the pointer swings round to 'Fair'.

If you really want to know what the weather is going to be like, however, it is much better to listen to the weather forecasts on the radio or television. Air pressure is affected by many things, and low pressure may bring wind, rain, snow, sleet, hail, thunder, lightning or any mixture of these. A barometer cannot tell you exactly what is coming, or when, and so can be used only as a very general guide.

Who discovered electricity?

Electricity — the name of which comes from the Greek word for amber — was first properly studied by Dr William Gilbert, the physician of Queen Elizabeth I. Though Dr Gilbert made many discoveries about the properties of electricity, neither he nor any other single man can be said to have discovered it. Many people, from ancient times to the present day, have each found out a little more about its nature and discovered ways in which it can be used.

Electricity was known to the women of ancient Syria, whose distaffs of amber became charged with it as they spun thread for their looms. This was the same kind of magnetic electricity that you can produce by running a plastic comb through your hair.

The old Chinese knew about the magnetic properties of lodestone. Two early Greek thinkers, Thales and Theophrastus, who lived respectively five hundred and three hundred years before Christ, studied the magnetic properties of amber. Aristotle (384—322 B.C.) studied the powers of a fish — probably the electric catfish, which, like the electric eel, was able to stun other creatures with a powerful shock. Seventy years after Christ, the Roman writer, Pliny, was investigating the electricity in amber.

An Englishman named Robert Boyle (1627—1691) discovered that electricity could be stored. A German scientist named Otto von Guericker, who lived at the same time as Boyle, made the first electric lamp by spinning a ball of sulphur and rubbing it with his hand, the friction of the hand causing the sulphur to glow in the dark.

After that, many men each discovered a little more. Sir Isaac Newton (1642—1727) — the man who discovered gravity — used a glass rod to pick up bits of paper. Francis Hawksbee, in the early 1700s, showed how electric sparks resemble lightning. At the same time, Stephen Gray was discovering that some materials conduct electricity, while others do not.

In the eighteenth century, discoveries were made in fast succession. In Holland, a professor called Musschenboek, made the Leyden jar, in which a strong charge of electricity could be built up. This invention was improved upon by an English scientist, Sir William Watson, who also proved that electricity travels so fast as to be instantaneous in its action.

In 1752, an American, Benjamin Franklin, proved that lightning is electricity by bringing some down from the sky along the string of a kite. John Canton (born 1718) made artificial magnets. Robert Symmer discovered the positive and the negative properties of electricity. Henry Cavendish (1731—1810) showed that iron wire was an excellent conductor of electricity, and by electrifying oxygen and hydrogen, turned the two gases into water.

While Cavendish was doing this in England, two Italian scientists, Luigi Galvani and Alessandro Volta, were also working hard. Volta (from whose name we get 'volt') made the first electric battery. Galvani (hence 'galvanise') investigated electric current after finding that dead frogs would kick when touched by an electrical contact.

Sir Humphry Davy (1778—1829) made the electric arc-lamp, forerunner of our modern electric lamps. Davy's assistant, Michael Faraday (1791—1867) invented the electric dynamo. James Clerk-Maxwell followed Faraday and made discoveries which helped Marconi develop wireless-telegraphy.

Thomas Alva Edison, together with Joseph Wilson Swan, invented the modern electric lamp. So the list goes on, right up to the present moment. And it will keep going on for many years yet, for the story of electricity is by no means ended.

What is a mammal?

Mammals are the most intelligent and advanced class of all the creatures that inhabit the earth. *You* are a mammal, the most intelligent of all the mammals. Your dog is another, not quite so advanced. The kangaroo is another, quite low in the scale. At the bottom is the duck-billed platypus.

A mammal is a warm-blooded animal, generally covered with hair, has a backbone, and suckles its young. With the exception of primitive egg-laying mammals like the duck-billed platypus, the young are born alive. The class covers a surprising number of creatures, ranging in size from the tiny pigmy shrew to the giant whale. Horses, cows, sheep, pigs, deer, lions, tigers, bears, wolves, elephants, bats, anteaters, armadillos, rats and mice . . . these are just a few of the great family.

Man belongs to the order of mammals known as the *Primates*, the most intelligent group, which includes the apes, monkeys, and lemurs.

What is the meaning of October?

October, like September, bears its old name which is two months out of date. It means 'the eighth month' but it is, of course, the tenth. The Anglo-Saxons used to call it 'the Yellow Month'.

What is caviare?

Caviare is the eggs, salted and dried, of the sturgeon. The sturgeon is a primitive, bony fish, between 2.5 and 3.5 metres long, which is found in many parts of the world, but especially in Southern Russia. It lives mainly in the sea, but is also found in fresh water. Some have been known to live two or three hundred years. Caviare, which is probably of Turkish origin, has been eaten as a delicacy since the sixteenth century. It is difficult to make, and even more dificult to keep, which is why it is so expensive. The fish itself is also a delicacy and can be eaten fresh or smoked.

What is money?

Long ago, people used to trade by barter: they 'swopped' things, just as you swop comics and toys with your friends. Barter, however, was a slow and clumsy process: it meant that traders had to carry great wagon-loads of goods about with them. They speeded things up a little by using less bulky objects, like measures of gold or silver, to exchange for other goods. Then, seven hundred years before Christ, the Lydians of Asia Minor, began to make coins of fixed value as tokens of exchange. Coins of gold, silver and copper lasted right up to 1914 when, for the first time in Europe, paper money was issued in large quantities. (There had been issues of paper money before this in the United States.)

Paper money itself — and, indeed our present-day coins — are not valuable in themselves, but their value is only in what they can be exchanged for. So a country would not get rich simply by printing lots of paper money. If there were not a lot of goods being produced to be exchanged for this money, the money would be worthless.

175

How does a fan keep you cool?

If the air around us is still, the heat from our bodies very soon warms it up. When the air becomes as warm as we are, our bodies can lose no more heat and we become hot and uncomfortable. If, however, we fan ourselves, the air is disturbed: the warm air is whisked away and cooler air is brought in to replace it. Thus we can go on losing heat and feel cool and fresh.

5TH OCTOBER

What was the Round Table?

The Round Table was the table at which, according to the legends written in the Middle Ages, King Arthur and his knights dined and talked. It was round to avoid any quarrels about which knights were more important than others. The story of the Round Table, like many other fanciful things in the Arthurian legends, is not true. There *was* an Arthur, but he was not a king, though he had royal blood in his veins. He was a Welsh soldier, probably half-Roman, who fought to keep out the Saxons after the Roman legions left Britain in the fifth century A.D. After his death, the story reached France and was brought back by the Normans. These stories of knights in armour, chivalry, fair maidens, jousting and quests were read by Sir Thomas Malory and re-written by him as *Morte d'Arthur*, printed by William Caxton in 1485.

What are clouds?

NIMBUS

Clouds are fogs or mists formed some distance above the ground. Made up of tiny drops of water floating in the air, they are caused by the cooling of air containing water vapour. There are four main types of cloud: *Cirrus* (which means 'wisp') *Cumulus* (heap) and *Stratus* (sheet) — the names of these describe their shape — and *Nimbus,* the black and shapeless rain cloud.

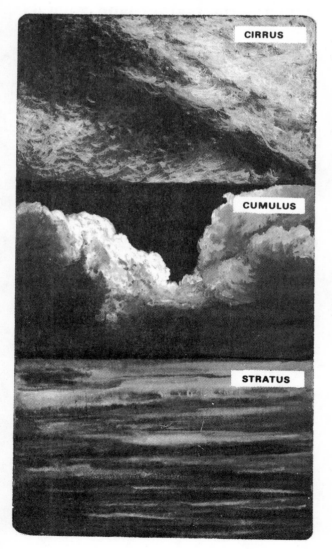

CIRRUS

CUMULUS

STRATUS

Do plants sleep at night?

Plants have no eyes to shut, no muscles to relax, but like us they still need sleep. They get it, as we do, at night. During the day the plant is busy, making food and new growth with the help of the sun. When darkness falls, the plant can no longer use the sun for its work. So it goes to sleep. Work stops, growth stops, and the plant waits for morning to start all over again.

What is the Black Forest?

Germany has many fine forests: more than a quarter of the land is covered with trees. The most famous of the forests is perhaps the Schwarzwald, or Black Forest, a mountain range in West Germany, where the border meets those of France and Switzerland. The mountain slopes are covered with dark-leaved fir trees, which give the forest its name.

Many German folk tales come from the region, and many wooden toys, instruments and clocks are made there, and it is a favourite holiday resort.

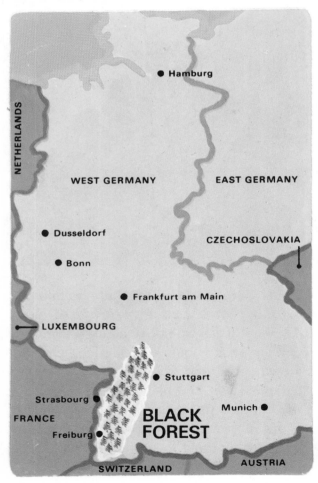

Which is the fastest land animal?

The cheetah, found in Africa and Asia, is a curious creature. It is a member of the cat family, but has claws like a dog. It is also the fastest animal on land, being capable of speeds up to seventy miles an hour over short distances. In India it is often trained to hunt deer.

What is a fungus?

Fungi are a large group of very simple plants. Unlike higher plants they are not green. They include toadstools, mushrooms, moulds, mildews, rusts (the 'rusts' on plants, not on metals) and yeasts. Their bodies, except in the case of yeast, are made of a tangled mass of fine hairs which burrow into the dead animal or vegetable matter on which they live. Unlike higher plants, they do not have the green colouring called *chlorophyll*. (Some moulds are green, it is true, but the colouring comes from a different pigment.) They reproduce by spores, tiny 'seeds' which are carried by the air until they find a suitable place to grow. The mushrooms we see are not the whole of the fungus, or anywhere near it. They have only popped up out of the ground to release the spores. The real plant is in the threads underground. Fungi, though they cause many diseases among plants, and some among animals, are essential to life because they break down all kinds of dead matter into material that other plants can use.

What does 'circus' mean?

'Circus' comes from the Latin word for a ring, or circle. In ancient Rome it was the circular arena built for holding chariot and horse racing, games, gladiatorial combats and fights between wild beasts. From these bloodthirsty beginnings has come our circus of today, still with a ring, but with much pleasanter things going on inside it.

Who was Siegfried?

Siegfried was the hero of several legends of Germany and Scandinavia, but he is most famous today as one of the main characters in Wagner's cycle of four operas called 'The Ring of the Nibelung', which is based on those legends.

In Wagner's version, some dwarfs, called the Nibelung, have taken treasure from the Rhine and forged it into a magic ring. Whoever owns this ring will control the world, but it is stolen from the Nibelung by a dragon called Fafner. The fearless Siegfried kills the dragon with a magic sword, and takes the ring. Then he rescues Brunnhilde, a beautiful maiden who has displeased the gods, and gives the ring to her.

Meanwhile, Hagen, the son of one of the Nibelung, is plotting to recover the ring.

He and his half-brother, Gunther, give Siegfried a drink which makes him forget Brunnhilde. Wearing a magic helmet which makes him seem like Gunther, he persuades Brunnhilde to become Gunther's wife. But when she sees Siegfried, who cannot remember her, she is furious, and tells Hagen and Gunther to kill him. Then she learns the truth of how Siegfried was tricked, and rides into the fire where his body is being burnt, to die with him. The River Rhine overflows, putting out the fire and carrying away the ring, which is lost for ever.

Wagner wrote his operas at a time when Germany was a very new country, and the people were interested in their own folk-stories which showed that they had traditions as long as those of any older nation. Bismarck made Germany into an Empire in 1871 *(see 4th February)*, and Wagner's operas based on these folk-stories were first produced in 1876, so they have always been very popular in Germany.

What is dew?

When the sun goes down and night falls, the air becomes much colder than it was during the day. The cold causes the water vapour in the air to condense — that is, to turn back into water. These tiny drops of water fall back to the ground and collect on cold, exposed surfaces, like stones or blades of grass, to form the bigger drops we see early in the morning as dew.

14TH OCTOBER

What happened in 1066?

On October 14th, 1066, was fought the Battle of Hastings, a battle which marked the last successful invasion of England, and changed the course of the country's history.

William, Duke of Normandy, had been promised the throne of England by his cousin, Edward the Confessor. After the Confessor's death, however, the Witan, or king's council, chose Harold, Duke of Wessex, instead.

The outraged William landed with an army of Normans at Pevensey, while Harold was in the north defeating an invading army of Vikings. Harold and his tired army hurried south, and met William at Senlac Hill, about six miles outside Hastings. In a fierce battle, the entire Saxon army was destroyed, including Harold himself.

This left the way open for William to conquer the rest of England — though such was the Saxon hatred of the Norman that it took him more than twenty years to do it.

What is an oasis?

An oasis is a water hole in the desert which enables plants to grow and men and animals to drink. It may be merely a small spring, supporting a few palm trees, or it may be quite a large lake, around which men can settle and grow crops. Oases are very important to the nomads, or wandering herdsmen, in desert areas, who take their flocks from one to the other. Even today there are tribal wars in places like Ethiopia over possession of oases.

What is asbestos?

Asbestos is a mineral found in certain rocks. When it is rubbed, it breaks up into silky threads which can be woven into cloth. Shorter threads can be pressed together into sheets or shaped in moulds. Asbestos is very useful to us because it is not affected by fire or chemical action: your mother may have an asbestos mat in the kitchen on which she stands hot dishes, or a pair of asbestos mittens for lifting things from the oven. Fire-fighting suits, which enable a fireman to walk right into the heart of a blaze, are also made from asbestos. Asbestos cement, made by soaking the fibres with cement, is used for roofing sheds and garages and making outside drainpipes.

What is a quicksand?

A quicksand is a very loose sand, mixed with lots of water, in which heavy objects sink very easily. The sand does not stick together under pressure, as do ordinary sands, and is therefore a very dangerous thing to walk on. If you are out walking by a river mouth — which is where they are mostly found — take notice of any warning boards. Never go walking alone in a quicksand area. And if you should be unlucky enough to get caught in one, do not struggle — this makes sinking all the quicker. Get your friend to run for help or to reach out with a stick so that you can pull yourself clear.

Where does the rainbow get its colours?

White light is really made up of seven different colours: red, orange, yellow, green, blue, indigo and violet. It can be split up into these colours by a specially shaped piece of glass called a prism—you may have seen this in experiments at school. It is these spectral colours which give the rainbow its gay appearance. Sunlight, shining through raindrops in the air, is split up to form the coloured arch we all know so well. You may see rainbows in your garden, caused by the sun shining through the spray of father's lawn-sprinkler.

183

What does gravity mean?

The theory of gravity was worked out by Sir Isaac Newton (1642—1727). One day he saw an apple falling off a tree to the ground. He wondered why it should do this, and realised that there must be a force inside the earth, pulling towards it all objects upon and around it.

When we let go of something and it falls to the ground, it is gravity which has pulled it there. It is gravity which holds us to the earth and stops us floating away into space.

There is a similar force working on each planet and on the sun, as we read earlier.

'Gravity' comes from the Latin word meaning 'heavy'. What happens when there is no gravity is seen in the state of weightlessness experienced by astronauts: they, and everything else which is not fixed to the walls of their cabin, float around quite freely in mid-air.

20TH OCTOBER

What is a dyke?

The word 'dyke' has a double meaning: it is either a wall built to keep out the sea, as in Holland, or a deep wide ditch dug to drain the land, as in the fen country of England. Its double meaning is not curious when you realise that the word once meant a defensive earthwork, consisting of both a wall and a ditch.

Napoleon to invade Egypt. In 1801 he defeated the Danish fleet and made the Danes agree not to fight for Napoleon. For this he was made a viscount. On October 21st, 1805, Nelson met the French fleet at the battle of Trafalgar, off the coast of Spain. His flagship *Victory* — which can be seen still at Portsmouth — was engaged by several enemy ships and Nelson was shot by a French marksman as he stood on the deck. Carried below, he died from his wound — but not before he knew that he had won the day. Trafalgar Square, in London, was laid out and named to commemorate the battle, and a 44-metre-high column, topped with a 5.5-metre statue of Nelson himself, was erected in memory of the great admiral.

21ST OCTOBER

What is the column in Trafalgar Square?

Admiral Viscount Horatio Nelson was the greatest seaman Britain ever produced. Born in Norfolk, in 1758, he first went to sea at the age of twelve. At twenty-one, he became a captain. Nelson fought in many sea battles and quickly got a reputation for courage. He lost an eye in one engagement and his right arm in another. At the Battle of St Vincent, in 1797, Nelson disobeyed his commander's orders by putting his telescope to his blind eye when reading a signal. His disobedience helped the British to win, and he was made a rear-admiral and knighted. In 1798 he destroyed, at Aboukir Bay, the French fleet sent by

How does blood flow?

Strictly speaking, blood does not flow — it is *pumped* around the body by the heart. The heart is a very strong hollow bunch of muscles. When it squeezes the blood inside it — and you can hear this action as a heart-beat — the blood is forced into stiff tubes called *arteries* which carry it to all parts of the body. From the arteries the blood flows into fine, hair-like tubes called *capillaries,* which take it to all the organs of the body. After doing its work in the different parts of the body, the blood flows through more capillaries into large, limp tubes called *veins,* which lead back to the heart. This journey by the blood around the body is called circulation. Circulation was discovered by the English doctor, William Harvey, after experiments in 1628.

22ND OCTOBER

What is a pendulum?

A pendulum is a weight, fixed to a rod, which is allowed to swing from side to side. The curious thing about it is that, once it is put in motion, its beat is regular, no matter how long or short the swing is. It was invented by the great Galileo (1564—1642) who was inspired by watching the swinging of a lamp in the cathedral at Pisa. He used it to measure the human pulse and it was, in fact, the first mechanical device to help doctors in their diagnosis of illness.

You may have seen a pendulum on a clock, keeping regular time: this is perhaps its most common use, but it has many others. The French scientist Foucault used one in an experiment to show the rotation of the earth. It is also used in certain measuring experiments and in machinery.

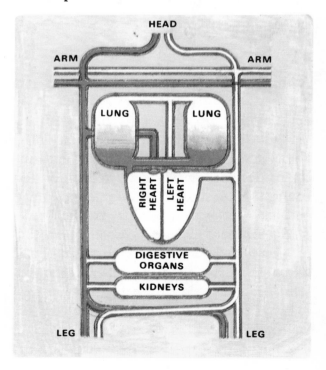

What is the United Nations?

The United Nations is an organisation of countries who would rather talk over their differences than fight about them. It was formed in 1945 by the Allied powers who, after the Second World War, were determined that such a dreadful and destructive struggle should not take place again. It began with fifty members: now there are one hundred and forty-one. It meets in New York in a large skyscraper built for it by the American Government.

Although it has no permanent army, it can call upon troops of member countries to put down outbreaks of fighting in the countries of other members. It collects no taxes, but relies on members' contributions to pay for the things it does.

It has many activities, including helping poorer countries to fight disease and starvation. The ideals of the United Nations were written down in the United Nations Charter, first published on October 24th, 1945. This day is now observed all over the world as United Nations Day.

There was an organisation called the League of Nations, set up between the world wars, which had the same aims. It failed, however, because members could not agree among themselves, and because several important countries either did not join or resigned from it. It is important for every one in the world today that the United Nations does not suffer the same fate.

187

What is a coral reef?

An animal called a *polyp,* which looks like a plant and which lives in warm salt water, builds itself a skeleton from the lime it collects from the sea. This skeleton is as hard as rock and protects the polyp during its lifetime. When the polyp dies, the skeleton remains, and other polyps come along, anchor themselves, and build further skeletons. These skeletons are coral. Over thousands of years, in a spot where millions of polyps have been living together as a colony, the layers of coral have built up into a great wall, or reef, which at low tide reaches to the surface of the sea. Some reefs are very big indeed: the Great Barrier Reef, off the north-east coast of Australia, for instance, is about 1,000 miles long.

25TH OCTOBER

What is steam?

You have never seen steam — not real steam, that is. The cloud you see coming from the spout of your kettle, or from the funnel of a steam engine, is a cloud of water droplets. True steam is made when water is heated so much as to become an invisible gas. If you look near the spout of your kettle — be careful, mind — you will see a gap before the cloud of visible steam starts. This gap is the true steam, intensely hot and invisible, before the air has a chance to cool it and turn it back into water.

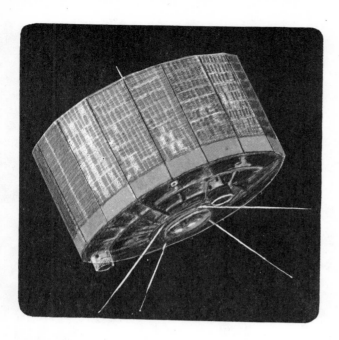

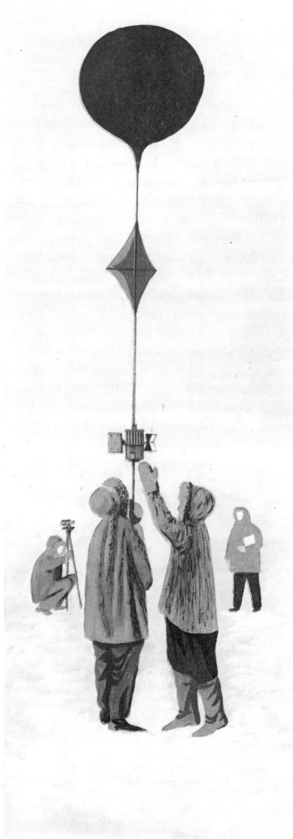

How does the weather forecaster know next week's weather?

The weather forecaster today is part of a world-wide network of people who pass on what they know about the weather in their own part of the globe. In this way a weather forecaster can plot wind-speed, temperatures cloud formations, air pressure, and so on, over a large area, and can work out from this what kind of weather is likely to come his way. The World Meteorological Association was set up in 1950 to help weather men of different countries to share their knowledge. Many scientific instruments are used to help the weather forecaster. Balloons and aircraft bring back news of winds, temperatures and clouds high up in the sky. Radar is used to track rain clouds. And there are even weather satellites in orbit round the earth, sending back reports to scientists on the ground.

What is a shooting star?

A shooting star, or meteor, is a lump of stone or metal, nobody knows where from, which whirls through space, burning up as it enters the earth's atmosphere, and leaving a short bright trail of glowing gas.

Millions of these are constantly bombarding our atmosphere, and most fizzle away. On a clear night, though, you might see about six. Most are very small, a fraction of an inch across, but some are so big that they hit the earth before they burn out. One landed in Mexico and exploded, leaving a crater 1280 metres wide and 174 metres deep. Others have remained whole. There is a mass of stone in South West Africa which weighs almost sixty tonnes. An iron one in America is three metres long and two metres high.

When were the first newspapers printed?

In the late 1500s and the early 1600s people got news of the outside world from printed broadsheets. These were not printed regularly, however, nor could the news in them always be relied on. In 1621, one of the broadsheets started coming out weekly, and this could be regarded as the beginning of newspapers.

The first daily newspaper, however, *The Daily Courant*, did not appear on the streets of London until 1702. And many people consider the first really good newspaper was *The Review*, started by Daniel Defoe, the author of 'Robinson Crusoe', in 1704.

After this several more newspapers were published, and the editors were often in trouble because the Governments of the day did not like being opposed in print.

The Times was founded by John Walter in 1785, and *The Daily Telegraph* came into being in 1855. Both of these exist today. Newspapers really began to flourish round about 1890. The Education Act of 1870 had enabled many more people to learn to read, and many newspapers were published to meet the demand. Today, with radio and television bringing news into the home, the demand for newspapers has fallen.

30TH OCTOBER

What is smell?

The lining of our noses is covered with nerve endings which are sensitive to little bits of matter which float about in the air. When we smell something — say, a strong cheese — it means that tiny particles of cheese are floating in the air, and touching the nerve endings in our nose. Messages go back along the nerves to the brain, which identifies that particular smell as cheese.

191

31ST OCTOBER

What is Hallowe'en?

Hallowe'en is October 31st, the day before the old Christian feast of All Saints or All Hallows, on November 1st. The customs we in Britain and America associate with Hallowe'en are even older than Christianity. The parties where people eat nuts and apples, and dress up as witches and black cats, can be traced back both to Roman times and to festivals in Britain where the Druids, the strange priests who used to use Stonehenge, would celebrate the end of summer, and the beginning of winter, the 'dead' season. Some of the old customs, like lighting bonfires, we now celebrate a few days later, on Guy Fawkes' night.

What is the meaning of November?

November, the eleventh month in our calendar, means 'ninth month' — it is another name from the old calendar which has not been altered, though its place in the year has been moved. November, to our Anglo-Saxon ancestors, was *Blotmonath*, or 'Blood Month', when they killed off the animals they could not feed during the winter.

2ND NOVEMBER

Which is the longest river in the world?

The Nile, the great river of Africa which gives life to Egypt and the Sudan, is the longest single river in the world, with a length of 4,160 miles.

The second longest river is the Amazon, which is 3,900 miles long. However, if you count all the tributaries, or measure the area it drains, then the Amazon is the *biggest* river in the world. Its tributaries cover the whole of Brazil and come also from Bolivia, Peru, Colombia and Ecuador.

The Yangtze-Kiang, the longest river in China, is the world's third longest *single* river, with a length of 3,100 miles. The combined lengths of the Mississippi and Missouri rivers in the United States is 5,064, miles, and they are often spoken of as a single river. As the Missouri does not flow into the Mississippi until about half-way down its length, however, the longest continuous flow is only 3,710 miles. The Missouri is 2,714 and the Mississippi 2,350 miles long. Africa's second longest river is the Congo, with a length of 2,718 miles.

	1,000	2,000	3,000	4,000
NILE				
AMAZON				
YANGTSE-KIANG				
CONGO				
MISSOURI				
MISSISSIPPI				

How does a boomerang return?

The boomerang, the hunting weapon of the Australian aborigine, is a curved piece of hard wood, about 76 centimetres long, flat on one side and rounded on the other. A slight twist in the angle of one of the 'wings' makes it return to the owner when thrown — unless, of course, it hits something on the way. Not all boomerangs come back: there are special non-returning types made for use in warfare.

3RD NOVEMBER

What is a thunderbolt?

Even today many people think that the thunderbolts — large masses of stone or iron — fall from the sky during a thunderstorm. It is true that, after a bad thunderstorm, objects have been found buried in the soil where lightning has struck. And these *are* thunderbolts — but they have not fallen from the sky. They have been caused by lightning striking a sandy soil and melting the rock particles in it to form a tube-shaped object. Small meteorites and other bits of stone have also been claimed as thunderbolts, but though the meteorite *has* fallen from the sky, it was not brought by thunder.

How are fireworks coloured?

Man has been using fireworks for thousands of years. They had their beginnings, like many other things, in China, and gradually spread through the East. They were probably brought to Europe by the Crusaders in the thirteenth century. The colours in fireworks are produced by putting metal salts in the explosive: copper makes blue, barium green, sodium yellow and strontium red.

6TH NOVEMBER

What is a desert?

A desert is any region in which little life can exist because of shortage of water or intense cold. The second kind of desert is worth remembering, because most people think of deserts only as scorchingly hot places. A desert comes into being when the annual rainfall is below about 25cms. Man has helped to make many deserts, either by allowing his animals to eat all the vegetation, and so let the sun dry up the earth, or by farming so badly that the wind blows the fertile topsoil away, leaving only dust in which little will grow.

The big hot deserts of the world are found in Africa, North and South America, and Australia. The cold deserts are found mainly in Asia and in Arctic and Antarctic regions.

What are artificial satellites?

Artificial satellites are man-made space vehicles which have been put into orbit around either the earth or some other planet. These satellites are generally fitted with equipment to radio back to earth information about conditions in space. The first artificial satellite of all was the Russian Sputnik I, which was put into orbit on October 4th, 1957. Sputnik I was followed by Sputnik II, and then in February, 1958, by the American Explorer I. Since then, many artificial satellites have been put into orbit and scientists have even discussed the possibility of space travellers in the future being put into danger by the presence of so much orbiting 'scrap iron'.

Who were the Wright Brothers?

Orville and Wilbur Wright were two American brothers who made the world's first controlled flights in a powered aeroplane. On December 17th, 1903, at Kitty Hawk, North Carolina, the brothers made four flights between them in their No. 1 *Flyer*. Orville (1871—1948) made the first flight at a height of between 2.5 and 3.5 metres and an airspeed of thirty to thirty-five m.p.h. It lasted just twelve seconds. The best flight was made by Wilbur (1867—1912) who stayed in the air for fifty-nine seconds at a speed of just over thirty m.p.h. The brothers went on to build better aircraft. On October 4th, 1905, their No. 3 *Flyer* stayed in the air for a full thirty-eight minutes, covering twenty-four miles. Other pioneers followed their lead and within a few years the Air Age was well under way.

What is an element?

When you think of all the many different things in the world — mountains, rivers, animals, plants, rocks, metals, solids, liquids, gases — it would appear that to make all these things nature must be using an untold number of different materials. In fact, all these things, including you yourself, are made up of one or more elements, of which there are only a hundred and three different kinds.

An element, then, is the basic building material of our world. It cannot be changed into anything else. All its atoms are of one type and cannot be turned into anything else by chemical means.

The reason there are so many apparently different materials in the world is that elements can join together to make other substances. Water, for instance, is made up of the elements of oxygen and hydrogen. Sulphuric acid is made up of oxygen, sulphur and hydrogen.

Some elements with which you will be familiar are aluminium, copper, gold, iodine, iron, lead, mercury, silver, tin and zinc. Among the gaseous elements are hydrogen, helium, nitrogen and oxygen.

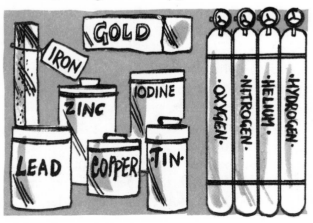

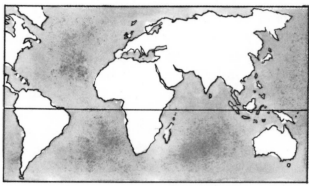

What is a map?

A map is a drawing of the earth's surface, or part of it, on a flat surface such as a sheet of paper, linen or parchment. A map can never be accurate, simply because it *is* on a flat surface, while the surface of the earth is curved. The only way the earth can be mapped properly is on a globe. Map-makers, or cartographers, transfer the curved surface of the globe on to a flat plane by means of a *projection*. There are several ways of projecting an area on to a map, depending on whether it is wanted to be correct for direction, area or shape. Perhaps the most famous projection of all is Mercator's, devised in 1568 by the German Gerhard

Kramer, or Gerardus Mercator. This projection is probably the one used in your school atlas. The trouble with it is that it makes the earth as wide at the poles as at the equator, enlarging quite small countries until they appear as big as continents.

The earliest mapmakers were the ancient Egyptians, who made their first attempts 1400 years before Christ. Their ideas were improved later by the Greeks, and in about A.D. 150 another Egyptian, Ptolemy of Alexandria, used lines of latitude and longitude, which prepared the way for our own modern maps, but most of the world was not yet known.

Making accurate maps is a very skilled job. There has been a great increase in accuracy since the invention of the camera, particularly since people began to take aerial photographs from planes and satellites, which show not only the outlines, but also the shape of the earth's surface.

What is Armistice Day?

On November 11th, 1918, at the end of the First World War, the Germans and General Foch, the French leader of the Allies, signed an agreement to stop fighting. This was called 'The Armistice'. Peace was negotiated at Versailles in 1919. Between the two World Wars, November 11th was kept as a day of remembrance for the soldiers who were killed in the war, and people wore Flanders poppies, which grow in Belgium, where much of the fighting took place. After the Second World War, November·11th was kept as Remembrance Day for both wars. Nowadays, Remembrance Day is always on the Sunday nearest November 11th. There are services at war memorials all over Europe.

What is a crystal?

A crystal is a substance which, when it turns solid, takes on a definite form or pattern. Crystals of the same substance, salt, for example, are peculiar in that they have the same number of faces and are the same shape whatever the difference in size may be. Most solid substances, when pure — that is, not mixed with other things — take on crystalline form.

Crystallisation can happen in three different ways. If you dissolve salt or sugar in water and let that water evaporate, crystals are left behind. When molten metal cools, the solid mass is made up of tiny crystals. The third kind of crystallisation happens when water vapour turns into snowflakes.

Who lives at the White House?

The White House, in Washington, is the official home of the President of the United States. A very English-looking house, rather like one of our country houses, it is built of stone and painted white, hence the name.

Its foundation stone was laid by George Washington and it was first occupied in 1800 by John Adams. In 1814, during the Anglo-American War, it was set on fire by British troops.

What do butterflies eat?

Butterflies feed on nectar, the sugary substance found at the base of flower petals. So that they can feed without damaging their wings by having to crawl into the flowers, they have a long tube through which they can suck up the nectar. When not in use, this tube is rolled tightly under the head.

15TH NOVEMBER

Why is Sir Humphry Davy so well-known to miners?

One of the greatest hazards in a coal mine is the presence of an explosive gas known to the miners as fire damp. The exploding of this gas by the naked lights used by the miners caused many dreadful accidents underground. A lamp which would not explode the gas was invented by Humphry Davy (later Sir Humphry) during the time, from 1801 to 1812, that he worked at the chemical laboratory of the Royal Institution in London.

The Davy Lamp, a version of which is still used today, has a cylinder of wire gauze around the flame. Any fire damp which gets through the gauze burns up — but the gauze quickly conducts the heat away so that the flame inside the cylinder cannot spread to the gas outside. This flaring up inside the cylinder is a warning to the miner that fire damp is present, so the lamp does double duty in helping to make the mine a safer place to work in.

201

Can a fish fly?

There are more than forty kinds of tropical fish which bear the general name of 'flying fish'. They have a pair of fins which have grown long and wing-like. With the aid of these fins they can leap out of the water and make fairly long, skimming flights to escape their enemies. This flight, however, cannot be controlled: the fish does not have muscles strong enough to enable it to flap the fins and gain height. So, although a fish cannot *fly* in the true sense, a flying fish can certainly *glide* well enough to stay alive for distance of about 45 metres.

Who formulated the Theory of Relativity?

The Theory of Relativity was formulated by Albert Einstein, born of Jewish parents in Germany in 1879. The Theory, which is a difficult one even for adults to grasp, was first worked out by Einstein in 1905 and later expanded by him into his General Theory of 1915. What Einstein did was to work out mathematically certain laws of light, energy and gravitation which changed the old ideas about the structure of the universe. Einstein stated, for instance, that light was 'bent' by gravitational attraction. This was proved right four years later by observations made during an eclipse of the sun. The importance of Einstein's Theory is that it enabled scientists to discard old ideas which had been leading their calculations astray, and to make great advances in their knowledge of the universe, leading man to the brink of space travel.

What is odd about a cuckoo?

Although the first song of the cuckoo is hailed with joy every year as a sign that spring has arrived, the bird has very little else to recommend it. It does not make a nest of its own, but lays its eggs, one at a time, in the nests of other birds, leaving these birds with the task of feeding and caring for its large and greedy baby. The poor foster-parents do not realise that there is a strange egg in the nest, for the cuckoo's egg is coloured to resemble whichever kind it is laid next to. The baby cuckoo is quite ruthless. The first thing he does when hatched is to throw out of the nest all the other baby birds or eggs.

19TH NOVEMBER

What is an abbey?

An abbey is a monastery of either monks or nuns, ruled over by an abbot or an abbess. Many of the great English churches which bear the name of 'Abbey' do so because they were originally attached to a monastery. Westminster Abbey, for instance, was once occupied by Benedictine monks and Fountains Abbey in Yorkshire by Cistercians. Most English abbeys fell into disuse when Henry VIII ordered the dissolution of the monasteries at the time of Reformation.

of our turning into a race of giants. A giant is anyone over two metres tall and though it might seem exciting to be as big as this, it is often the reverse. Most people who grow tall enough to be considered giants are quite sickly and die young. Their size is often due to the over-activity of the pituitary gland, which governs the rate of growth of our bones. Two famous giants were the Irishmen Cornelius McGrath and Charles Byrne. McGrath stood 2.6 metres and Byrne 2.4 metres. Much taller than either of them was the Russian giant Fedor Machnov, who was 2.8 metres tall.

21ST NOVEMBER

Can ants fly?

20TH NOVEMBER

What is a giant?

We are taller than our fathers were, and they were taller than theirs. Each generation adds a little to the general stature of the human race. But this is a slow process and will not go on for ever: there is little danger

Ants are the most intelligent of all insects. They live together in large colonies and each has its own job to do. Because different duties demand different strengths and skills, the bodies of ants in the same colony vary

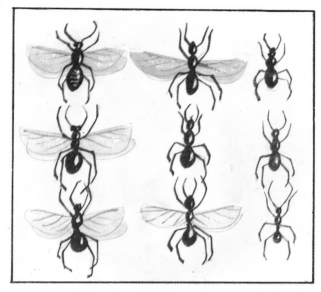

Who were the Brothers Grimm?

Many of our favourite fairy stories came originally from Germany, and people all over the world can enjoy them today because of the work of the Brothers Grimm.

Jacob Ludwig Grimm and his brother, Wilhelm Carl, were born within a year of each other, and lived and worked together all their lives. They were very learned men, who did a lot of important work on the German language. They were also very interested in the old German folk stories, which they collected and wrote down. They published their first collection in 1812. Some of those you will know are *Snow White and the Seven Dwarfs, Hansel and Gretel, Little Red Riding Hood* and *Rumpelstiltskin*.

according to their duties. So we get the worker ants who have no wings and whose job, as their name implies, is to do all the fetching, carrying and building of the colony. Then there are the queen ants and the males, both of whom have wings. These wings are used only for the mating flights, after which the queens bite off their own wings and settle down to laying eggs. The males, for whom there is no job after the nuptial flight, generally die very shortly afterwards.

How does a refrigerator work?

The most common kind of refrigerator is the type you have in your house and which you see, in larger forms, in butcher's shops and fishmongers. It is called a *vapour-compression* refrigerator. What happens is that a special fluid, usually ammonia, is pumped through pipes in the cold-chamber. The fluid draws heat out of this chamber to turn itself into a vapour. This vapour then flows along to a compressor, where it is turned back, by pressure, into a fluid. The fluid is then pumped into the cold chamber, and the whole cycle of events starts again.

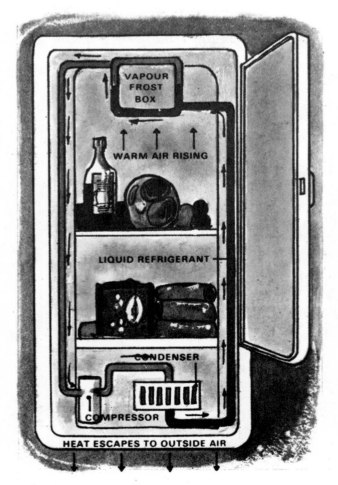

What is the Equator?

The Equator is a circle drawn round the globe, midway between the north and south poles, dividing the earth into two. Along this line the sun is directly overhead at noon at the equinoxes (March 22nd and September 22nd). It is from the Equator that we measure our lines of latitude, north and south. The Equator measures 24,902 miles in length and is the longest line which can be drawn round the earth. Crossing the Equator, or 'crossing the line' is always a great event on board passenger ships, and special ceremonies are held — usually involving the shaving and ducking of a passenger by a crew member dressed as King Neptune.

What is vaccination?

Vaccination is a way of preparing the body to resist disease by injecting it with a substance which makes it think it *has* the disease, and so making it produce *antibodies* to fight the infection. These antibodies stay in the bloodstream for some time — in some cases for life.

In 1721 Lady Mary Montagu brought from Turkey the practice of inoculating people with lymph, or fluid, from the rash caused by mild cases of smallpox. This actually gave the person smallpox but, because it was mild, it was not dangerous. So the patient survived and after that was immune to more serious forms of the disease common at the time.

In the west country of England, farmworkers who caught cowpox from their animals were found to be immune later from the more severe smallpox. This was learned, in 1796, by Edward Jenner, who began inoculating children with cowpox lymph to protect them from smallpox.

Since then, many diseases have been fought by vaccination, and vaccines have taken several forms. They can be mild forms of the disease (e.g. cowpox to provide immunity against smallpox); dead bacteria or viruses (e.g. those of typhoid, paratyphoid and poliomyelitis); germs treated to reduce their strength (e.g. the BCG vaccine for tuberculosis); or *antitoxins* to help fight diseases such as diphtheria and tetanus at short notice.

Without vaccination, many of you who are reading this would have died from one of the diseases which used to attack children not so very long ago.

Who were the Pilgrim Fathers?

In England, even after the Reformation, there were many people who felt that some practices in the Church were wrong. They were called 'Puritans' because they wanted to 'purify' the Church, but they criticised the king as well, so were unpopular with the government, who would not listen to their 'purifying' ideas.

So, in 1620, a group of Puritans set sail from Plymouth, in the ship *Mayflower*, bound for New Jersey, but bad weather forced them to land at Massachusetts, where they founded a colony, which they called Plymouth. The first winter was very severe and many of the colonists died, but those who survived struggled to carve a living out of the surrounding forests, and were the basis of the population of the area which came to be known as 'New England'.

In the United States today, the Pilgrims are still thought of as the Founding Fathers of the nation. Every year, the third Thursday in November is kept as Thanksgiving Day in remembrance of the safe gathering of the harvest after their first year. On the first Thanksgiving Day, friendly Indians showed the colonists how to mash squash and catch wild turkeys which are still traditional Thanksgiving food.

What is respiration?

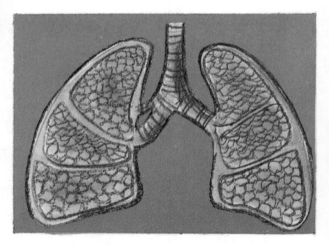

Respiration is the process by which oxygen is taken to the blood, and carbon dioxide and water vapour taken out of it — in other words, breathing. We discussed earlier, on January 28th, the work of lungs in land animals and gills in fish in performing this

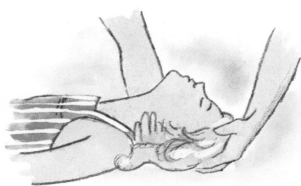

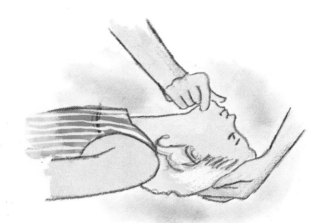

very important function. Perhaps in First Aid you have learned to give artificial respiration to somebody who has been pulled out of the water. What you are doing here is to get the lungs working again by doing the job which the diaphragm does in normal breathing. The diaphragm is a strong muscle across the bottom of the rib-cage. When you breathe out, you tighten this muscle, so that you squeeze the air out of your lungs. When you breathe in, there is a bigger area inside your ribs, because the diaphragm drops, so air goes in through your nostrils to fill it.

Another kind of artificial respiration, illustrated here, is the 'mouth to mouth' method.

Why is a cat's tongue rough?

If you have ever been licked by a cat you will have noticed how rough its tongue is. This roughness is caused by hard pieces of skin between the taste buds on the surface of the tongue, and it is there for a reason. In the wild, an animal has to make the most of every scrap of food it can find, and the rough tongues of the cat family — lions and tigers are just the same — help their owners to scrape the last bit of meat from the bones of their prey. The roughness is also useful in keeping the cat clean: watch your pet at its careful and regular grooming and notice how the tongue acts as brush and comb as well as a flannel.

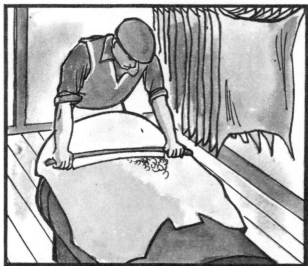

29TH NOVEMBER

How is leather made?

The raw material of leather is the skin, or hide, of an animal such as the cow or horse. First, it is scraped clean of all the bits of fat and flesh on the inside, and then the hair is taken off from the outside. What is left is a clean skin, but one which would soon rot if left untreated. The treatment it gets is called 'tanning'. The two most common forms of tanning are vegetable, or bark, tanning and chrome tanning.

In vegetable tanning the hides are soaked in a brew of *tannin* obtained from certain barks. They are transferred to stronger and stronger brews until the process is complete. Then they are steeped in dye and finally given a dressing of a mixture of soap and oil called a fat-liquor to make the leather soft and workable. In chrome tanning, the process is much the same except that chromium compounds are used instead of bark. Chrome leather has the advantage over vegetable-tanned leather in that it is not affected by boiling water.

After tanning, the leather is 'finished', to give it a good surface.

What is heredity?

Heredity is the name given to the fact that we, and all living things, inherit certain characteristics from each of our parents.

In the 1860s, an Austrian monk, Gregor Mendel, discovered the principles of how heredity works by crossing different varieties of garden pea. He found that each 'parent' would pass on its characteristics in *genes*, but which characteristics were inherited by the next generation depended on which parent's genes were stronger. The same principle applies to human beings, so if, for instance, one brown-eyed and one blue-eyed parent had four children, only one of the children would be likely to have blue eyes. The other three would probably have brown eyes, because brown eye genes are stronger than blue ones.

What is the meaning of December?

December is another month whose old name has stuck. It means, literally, the tenth month. But to us it means much more than that: it means parties, chestnuts and turkey and toys — and Christmas.

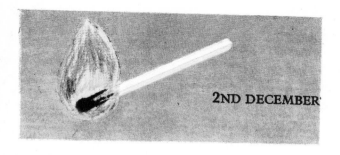

What are matches made of?

The head of a match is a mixture of things which will flare up together as soon as they get warm. This happens when the match is rubbed along the rough striking surface of the box. One substance, usually *potassium chlorate*, contains a lot of oxygen to help the other substance, *phosphorus sulphide*, to burn quickly with lots of heat. (There is usually some sulphur and charcoal in the match head too, to help the process along.)

In safety matches, the kind which will not strike on anything but their own box, the phosphorous is not in the match head but on the striking surface.

By the way, *don't* experiment with matches on your own. It looks safe enough, but very nasty accidents can happen.

What is the Grand Canyon?

In the high plateau of North Arizona, in the United States, is a gigantic gorge, cut into the rock by the Colorado River. This gorge — three hundred miles long, more than a mile deep and from four to eighteen miles wide — is the Grand Canyon.

It was first discovered by Spaniards of the Coronado Expedition in 1540. How they must have marvelled at the sight: the different layers of rock in the sides of the Canyon each glowing a different colour, — dull red, buff, green, pink, grey, chocolate-brown, purple, according to its mineral content — great peaks rising from the Canyon floor to finish off level with the feet of the explorers at the top; gorges within gorges, cut over thousands of years by the winding of the river.

Today the Canyon is a great tourist attraction, and a long stretch of it has been enclosed in a national park, to be preserved, just as it is, for all time. There is nothing else like it in the world.

Why don't the planets collide?

A planet is a satellite of a star, and the only planets we know of are the nine of our own solar system — though we can assume that our sun is not the only star in the universe to have planets revolving around it. We on earth do not collide with Jupiter or Mars or any of the others because of the fine balance which has grown over countless millions of years, by which each planet keeps to its own orbit, well out of the way of the others. It is remotely possible that the balance could be disturbed by an explosion of the sun, or some such happening, in which case collision *could* happen — but this possibility is so remote that it is hardly worth thinking about.

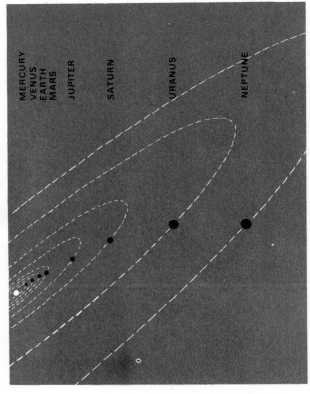

4TH DECEMBER

Which is the largest seabird?

The largest flying seabird is the albatross, whose 3.6-metre wingspan we discussed on April 5th. But if we count as seabirds those who use their wings for swimming and not for flying, the largest is the Emperor Penguin of Antarctica. Standing over 1 metre high and weighing 40 kilograms, the plump Emperors live in the most remote shores of the great ice-bound continent. Millions of years ago, there were much bigger penguins — fossils found in New Zealand show that they were giants indeed — but these died out.

Who was St Nicholas?

December 6th is the festival of St Nicholas — but nowadays we celebrate him on Christmas Day as Santa Claus, or Father Christmas.

The real St Nicholas was a bishop in Asia Minor, who died about A.D. 342. He became the patron saint of Russia and of children, sailors, merchants, and those in sudden danger.

There is a story about him which tells how one day he heard a man and his three daughters bewailing the fact that all their money was gone and that they would have to go out and beg to be able to buy food. Nicholas had three bags of gold, and two of these he put secretly, on two successive nights, through the window of the poor man. The man thought that the gold had come from God. On the third night he saw Nicholas put in the third bag of gold and fell at his feet.

Nicholas told him to give thanks to God. 'It was He who sent me to you,' he said.

This story, like many of the stories which attach themselves to saints, may or may not be true. But it certainly is a lovely tale and is one of the reasons we connect St Nicholas with the giving of presents at Christmas time.

215

What happened at Pearl Harbour?

On December 7th, 1941, Japanese aircraft and midget submarines attacked the United States naval base at Pearl Harbour, on the Hawaiian island of Oahu. Japan and America were not, up till then, at war. The attack took the American ships completely by surprise and much damage was done. After the attack, Germany and Italy, who were already fighting Britain, declared war on America, so bringing the United States into the Second World War.

8TH DECEMBER

How does a telephone work?

When you speak into a telephone mouthpiece, the sound you make causes a thin sheet of carbon — called a diaphragm — to vibrate. This vibration squeezes a collection of carbon grains packed behind the diaphragm. Flowing through these carbon grains is an electric current, and the alternate squeezing and letting go of the grains causes the strength of the current to change in time with this action.

The electric current flows away to the earpiece of the telephone held by the person you are speaking to. In this earpiece is a magnet, whose strength is altered by the 'flickering' of the electric current. The magnet sets up vibrations in another diaphragm in time with these flickerings, and these vibrations send out sound waves which hit the ear of the person you are speaking to.

So, briefly, you make sounds which are turned into an electric current, and the electric current is turned back into sounds.

As we read on February 18th, the telephone was invented in 1876 by Alexander Graham Bell, a Scotsman who went to live in America. He used an iron diaphragm set in front of a magnet for the mouthpiece, but the basic idea is still the same today.

9TH DECEMBER

What is the difference between a wasp and a bee?

Both bees and wasps are members of the insect order *hymenoptera,* which includes the ants. In many ways they are alike, but there are several big differences.

Wasps, in general, are slimmer, more brightly-coloured, and less hairy than bees. They can sting repeatedly, whereas the worker bee can only sting once. A bee's sting is barbed, and in withdrawing it the bee hurts itself so badly that it dies.

Bees make their nests of wax, and make honey to feed the little grubs. Wasps make their nests of paper and mud, feed their young on chewed-up insects or fruit, and do not make honey.

Bees are vegetarians. Many wasps are meat-eaters, killing spiders, flies and caterpillars.

Some bees are solitary, building a nest

by themselves, and rearing their young alone; other bees are social creatures and many thousands will share a nest or a hive. Wasps are divided, too, into solitary and social classes. The difference here is that the queen bee survives the winter in the nest with worker bees to look after her and to help her with the work of building and egg-laying in spring. The queen wasp, on the other hand, is the only one to survive the winter, and she has to build a new nest, lay her eggs and rear her young all by herself, until the youngsters grow big enough to take over some of the work.

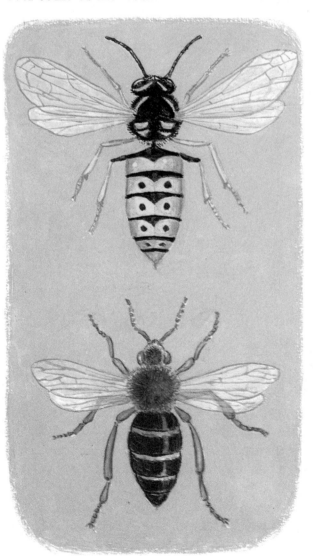

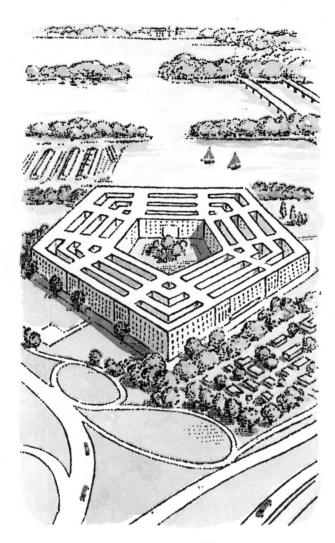

10TH DECEMBER

Is cotton a plant?

Cotton is indeed a plant, a small shrub belonging to the mallow family, which packs its seeds cosily in long white fibres inside a capsule. It is these fibres which are used to make our cotton thread and cloth. Man has cultivated the plant for so long that nobody really knows when he first did so. It was known to the ancients of the East — China, India and Egypt — and was also grown by the Incas of Peru before the coming of the Spaniards. Nowadays, most of the cotton we use is grown in the southern United States, Egypt, India and Pakistan.

Where is the Pentagon?

On the outskirts of Washington stands a five-sided building, called The Pentagon, which is the Greek word meaning 'five-sided'. In this building is the United States Department of Defence, which runs the army, navy and air force. If you see headlines in the newspaper saying 'Pentagon says so-and-so' or 'Pentagon does such-and-such', it means that the Department of Defence is doing or saying these things.

What is a catkin?

We are all familiar with the 'pussy willow', but many other trees besides the willow bear the strange flowers called catkins. Beech, hazel, polar, birch, walnut and sweet chestnut all carry them in the spring.

The flowers are strange because, unlike ordinary flowers which carry both the male and female parts — pollen-bearing stamens and ovaries — the catkin is either male or female, never both. Pollen from the male flowers is carried by the wind or by insects to the female ones, which then begin to produce seeds. When all the pollen has gone from a male flower, it dies and drops to the ground. Another peculiar thing about a catkin is the number and size of the flowers contained in a single one: masses of tiny flowers are packed together on one stalk, separated by small scaly leaves called bracts.

12TH DECEMBER

What is the North Pole?

The North Pole is the northernmost point of the earth, the 'top' of the world. At the opposite end is the South Pole. The earth spins on a line drawn between the North and South Poles called the 'axis'.

Locked eternally in ice and snow, the North Pole was first reached in 1909 by the American, Robert E. Peary. Some people doubted that Peary actually reached the Pole, but it seems fairly certain that he did. Since then the area around the Pole has been explored by other American, Canadian, British, Russian and Norwegian expeditions, but there is much important scientific work still to be done before we can really know much about the region.

Why is it that when a sheep falls over it cannot get up again?

Sheep are not the easiest of animals to look after: they are not very intelligent, to begin with, and have heavy bodies and delicate legs, which make them liable to all sorts of accidents.

Falling over and not being able to get up again is quite a common misfortune. When a sheep is on its back, it is weighted down by its thick, heavy fleece. Waving its legs about does not help, because they are too spindly and light to swing the body over their weight. So the poor old sheep has to wait for the shepherd to come and put him on his feet again.

15TH DECEMBER

What is a vulture?

A vulture is a large bird of prey which feeds mostly on animals which have died in the wild, or on the remains of prey left by other animals. There are two families of vultures: the *vulturidae* and the *cathartidae*. The second family is the American vulture, which is different in a few respects from those of the rest of the world.

Vultures are not very attractive, either in their appearance or in their way of life. They are generally bald on the head and neck, have long hooked beaks and untidy plumage. Their habit of soaring over dying beasts and then rapidly eating every morsel of flesh presented to them has led to them being regarded as symbols of death and greed — but they are very necessary in nature's balance of life: acting as the dustmen of the wild, clearing up carrion before it has a chance to rot away and spread disease.

The biggest vulture is the American condor, with a wingspan of nearly three metres, which can fly as high as three miles up. The condors and many others among the larger vultures, live to a great age — often fifty years or more.

16TH DECEMBER

What causes rain?

Warm air can hold a great deal of water vapour. When this air is cooled, by having to pass up over a range of mountains, for instance, into colder air, the vapour turns back to water. At first the water is in very tiny drops, which float in the air as clouds, fog or mist, but if the cooling process continues the drops join together to form larger drops. These larger drops are too heavy for the air to support, and they fall to the ground as rain. Rain can be caused artificially by sprinkling clouds with chemicals. Though this method is not really of much use to us at the moment, it is bound to be in the future.

COLD AIR

What is a sea knot?

Sailors measure the speed of their ships in knots, or nautical miles per hour. A nautical, or sea, mile is 1852 metres, longer than a land mile which is 1609 metres. The name comes from the old way of measuring speed by throwing overboard a log attached to a line, on which were knots at certain intervals. The line was paid out as the ship sailed on, and the speed worked out from the number of knots which appeared.

17TH DECEMBER

What is hail?

Hailstones are made by rain being blown *upwards* into even colder air, and freezing solid before dropping back to earth. Sometimes the hailstones are blown up several times before they finally fall, and when this happens they receive a fresh coat of ice each time, making really large stones.

Why is river water fresh?

River water is never *completely* fresh: it holds tiny quantities of minerals and salts washed from the rocks and soil. But these quantities are so small that we cannot taste them. A river generally starts its life as a spring, a bubbling out of water which has collected underground. When this water fell as rain it really *was* fresh: what minerals and salts it gathers on its journey as a river depends on the kind of rocks and soil it passes through.

19TH DECEMBER

What is a stalactite?

Water dripping from the roof of a limestone cave contains dissolved limestone, some of which is left behind after the drop has fallen. Over many years these tiny deposits of limestone build up to form a hanging column called *stalactite*. Growing up from the ground, built from limestone left by drops which have fallen from the stalactite, is often another column called a *stalagmite*. In time the two would meet to form one continuous column from floor to ceiling of the cave. The Cheddar Caves have some fine examples.

223

How is glass made?

Glass is made by fusing together, in a furnace, sand, soda and lime. This gives a liquid which can be cast as plate glass, moulded into containers such as jam jars, or blown by skilled men using long tubes into almost any shape. Today there are many different kinds of glass, made by using different materials, by cooling at different rates and by various other processes, but the basic methods and materials have remained much the same since glass-making was invented in Egypt more than fifteen hundred years before Christ. From Egypt the art spread to Europe and China. At first all glass vessels were moulded, but glass-blowing was invented in the first century B.C.

22ND DECEMBER

What is Stonehenge?

On Salisbury Plain, in Wiltshire, stand the ruins of a very mysterious prehistoric stone monument: Stonehenge. It consists of two circles of stones, one inside the other, and inside these are two horseshoe-shaped groups of stones, again one inside the other. The outer circle and outer horseshoe are of sandstone: the inner circle and inner horseshoe are of bluestones, which came originally from the Prescelly Mountains in Pembrokeshire, a hundred and eighty miles away. When you think that all this was erected about four thousand years ago, when travel was very difficult, you will appreciate what trouble the builders took. The plan of Stonehenge seems to show that it was built by sun-worshippers: at the summer solstice (June 21st) the open part of the horseshoe faces the sunrise and the sun shines on the altar stone inside the inner horseshoe.

23RD DECEMBER

What is a conifer?

Conifers are cone-bearing trees, and are the largest family of evergreens. The cones are the woody protective covering for the seeds — though they do not stop chisel-toothed animals like the squirrel from eating them.

The family includes fir trees, pines, spruces and cypresses. Though they are mostly evergreen, there are one or two exceptions, like the larch, which drop their leaves in winter. And though they are mostly quick-growing and soft-wooded, there are exceptions — like the yew — which are slow-growing and hard-wooded.

What is cork?

Cork is the thick, spongy bark of the cork oak, a tree which grows mainly in Portugal and Spain. Half the world's supplies come from Portugal, where the cork oaks are grown either in plantations or in natural forests. The trees are not very tall but have quite thick trunks, and about 20 kilograms of bark can be taken off at one stripping by a man using a sharp knife and a special axe. Stripping can only be done every ten years, so the growing of cork oaks is combined with farming. Often pigs are kept under the trees to root for the acorns which fall in autumn. When the cork is stripped it is boiled and then pressed to make the material we use in many ways, from medicine bottle stoppers to lifebelts.

25TH DECEMBER

What is the meaning of Christmas?

Christmas, or *Christ Mass,* is when we celebrate the birth of Jesus Christ. It was originally celebrated on January 6th, the date still observed by the Armenian Church, but in the fourth century A.D. the date of Christmas Day was changed to December 25th. This was a good time for the newly-converted heathens to celebrate Christ's birth, for the day marked the winter solstice, the shortest day of the year, and was a day on which many pagan gods were honoured.

There are several possible reasons why we give presents at Christmas: before Christianity came, offerings were made to heathen gods on December 25th; in the Bible story of the nativity, the three kings brought gifts to the infant Christ; and there is our old friend St Nicholas, whose date of present-giving — December 6th — was later transferred to the 25th.

26TH DECEMBER

Why is a skunk unpopular?

Poor old skunk — he's such a pretty animal, yet nobody loves him. He's unpopular because he smells. He doesn't smell all the time, but when he is frightened he squirts out an offensive liquid from two glands near his tail. It isn't just an ordinary smell — it's worse than any smell you can imagine. This keeps him safe from enemies in his home in open country in North and Central America, but it does not make him many friends.

The skunk also gets into trouble because, as a member of the weasel tribe, he is a meat-eater. In the wild he eats mice, frogs, birds' eggs and insects, but if he can find a hen-roost he will sneak in and make a feast of the occupants and their eggs.

He is a handsome fellow, slightly smaller than a cat, with a black coat set off by two white stripes which run along the back, and a long, bushy tail. Skunk fur is quite valuable.

Some people in America have taken to keeping skunks as pets — but only after the scent glands have been removed!

227

Who were the contestants in the American Civil war?

The United States of America is so called because it is made up of fifty separate little states, or countries, which run many of their own affairs but which act together as one big country in the more important matters such as taxation and defence.

At one time, in theory anyway, any state was free to leave, or secede from, the Union. But the American Civil War of 1861 to 1865 was sparked off when South Carolina announced that it was leaving the Union. Ten other Southern states joined South Carolina to form the Confederacy. The Southern politician, Jefferson Davis, set up his own government at Richmond, Virginia.

Opposing the secession of the Southern states was the Union, made up of Northern states, under President Abraham Lincoln.

The causes of the war were many and complicated. The only one people can be really sure of is the issue of slavery. The South, which depended on farming for its wealth, wanted to go on having slaves to work in the fields: the industrial North wanted to free them. There were twice as many people in the North as in the South, so if the Southern states stayed in the Union, the Northern states would always be able to make them do what they wanted.

So we have the two sides: the North, or Union, and the South, or Confederacy, fighting on the issue of whether the South could secede from the union, and keep slavery.

After a bitter struggle in which a million soldiers were killed, the North won.

The Southerners fought bravely, but the greater wealth and bigger armies of the North had their effect in the end. The North, too, had a stronger navy, with which it blockaded the Southern ports, preventing ships entering or leaving and so making it impossible for the South to send its cotton and tobacco overseas.

Why doesn't a spider get stuck in its own web?

The spider's web is made up of sticky silk-like threads, except for a small non-sticky platform in the middle where the spider waits for its prey. The reason the spider does not get tangled in its own web, when it leaves this centre platform, is that its legs are covered with a special oil which comes out of its body, and prevents the threads from sticking. This oil gives the spider complete freedom of movement over the whole of the web, so that when an insect gets trapped, the spider is able to shake the web to entangle it still further and then to rush out and bind its victim with so many criss-cross threads of silk that it cannot possibly escape.

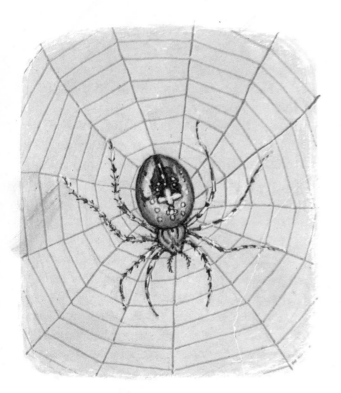

29TH DECEMBER

What is a spa?

Water in different parts of the country contains different amounts of mineral salts. Certain places have water which is rich in health-giving minerals, and people go to these places to bathe in, or drink, the water. A town to which people go for this reason is called a *spa*. The name comes from the town of Spa, in Belgium, one of Europe's oldest watering places.

Famous English spas include Bath, Buxton, Cheltenham, Leamington, and Malvern.

Why does a zebra have stripes?

The stripes of a zebra do not do much to camouflage it on the open African plains, especially as the zebras run in quite large herds which would be difficult to conceal even in thick forest. What the stripes do is make it difficult to tell one zebra from another, especially when they are running from a beast of prey. Because the stripes are broader on the rump and neck than they are on the rest of the body, they make these parts of the zebra seem nearer than the others. So a charging lion, as well as being confused by the mass of stripes in a zebra herd, can also be fooled into misjudging his distance from any particular animal.

31ST DECEMBER

What was Custer's Last Stand?

Lieutenant Colonel George Armstrong Custer was an American soldier who, by 1876, had become famous as an Indian-fighter. In the summer of that year, Custer and his regiment — five troops of the crack Seventh Cavalry — formed part of an expedition which had set out to round up the Sioux and Cheyenne Indians and drive them back to live on reservations.

In a valley by the Little Big Horn River in Montana Territory, Custer's scouts discovered an Indian camp. Custer, thinking there were a thousand Indians in the camp, ordered an attack. There were, in fact, 2,500 Indians, and in a fiercely-fought battle lasting only twenty minutes, Custer's entire force of 225 men — including Custer himself — was wiped out. The action became known as Custer's Last Stand.

After the battle the tribes broke up. And, though the Indians won the day, the Sioux and their allies never took to the warpath in force again.

INDEX

A

Abbeys, 203
Abraham, 40
Acorns, 106
Adders, 158
Aeroplanes, method of keeping aloft, 65
Aesop's Fables, 5
Albatross, 62—3, 214
Alligator, different from crocodile, 170
America, first discoverers of, 15
American Civil War, 228
    „   Independence Day (July 4), 119
Amoeba, An, 169
Animals, life span of, 120
    „   that change colour, 124
Ants, 204—5
April, meaning of, 60
Armistice (Remembrance) Day, 199
Ash Wednesday, 44
Athens, why so called, 12
Atomic energy, 152
August, meaning of, 136
Avalanches, 95
Aztecs, The, 13, 27

B

Balloons, why they rise, 36
Ballots, 146
Barometers, 171
Bastille Day (July 14), 125
Bats, how they 'see', 35
Beavers, 83
Bee, different from wasp, 217
    „ hives, 148
Bird, largest flying, 62—3
    „ , smallest, 150
    „ , largest sea, 214
    „ , migration, 45, 165
Birds, flightless, 100
    „ , warm-blooded, 158
Bird's eggs, colours of, 51
Black Forest, The, 178
Blood, circulation of, 186
    „ , human, 88
Bolivar, Simon, 149
Bone, composition of, 149
Boomerangs, 195
Braille alphabet, 62
Buckingham Palace, 83
'Buffalo Bill' (William Cody), 160
Buoys, 70

Butterflies, different from moths, 10
    „   , how they feed, 201

C

Calendars, 55
Camels' humps, 122
Carbon dioxide gas, 124
Castles, 16—17
Caterpillars, 84—5
Catkins, 219
Cats, tongues of, 210
Cavemen, Stone Age art, 10—11
Caves, 24
Caviare, 175
Cells, 160
Centipedes, 156
Charcoal, 99
Charlemagne, Emperor, 137
Charles I, only English king beheaded, 21
Cheeses, 94
Cheetah, fastest land animal, 178
Children's Crusade, The, 18
Christmas, meaning of, 226—7
Chromium, 81
'Circus', meaning of, 179
Clock, earliest, 80
Clocks, 24-hour system, 46
Clouds, 177
Coal, 132
Cocoa, 77
Colosseum, The (Rome), 140
Commons, House of, 157
Compass, working of, 134
Confucius (K'ung Fu-Tzu), 76
Conifers, 225
Continents, The, 126
Copper, 126
Coral reefs, 188
Cork oak tree, 6, 226
Corpus Christi, feast of, 104
Cotton plant, 218
Crocodile, different from an alligator, 170
Crusades, The, 168
Crustaceans, 28
Crystallisation, 200
Cuckoos, 203
Custer, Lt-Col George Armstrong, 230

D

D-Day, 101
da Vinci, Leonardo, 47, 102
Davy, Sir Humphrey, 201
Dead Sea, The, 159

December, meaning of, 212
Delphic Oracle, The, 73
Deltas, 77
Deserts, 196
Dew, 181
Domesday Book, 53
Don Quixote, 162
Dunkirk, 85
Dykes, 184

E

Eagle and snake, Mexico's flag, 27
Eagles as national emblems, 27, 154
Earth, distance from the sun, 118
    „   , rotation round the sun, 138
Earthquakes, 57
Echo, An, 130
Eiffel Tower, The, 144
Electric torch, working of, 76
Electricity, 92—3
    „   , discoverers of, 172—3
Elements, 198
Empire State Building, 84
Equator, The, 206

F

Fans, 176
February, meaning of, 23
Finger prints, 112
Fire, reason for heat of, 7
Fireworks, how colours produced, 196
Fish, breathing of, 74
    „ , 'flying', 202
    „ , hearing apparatus of, 43
    „ , method of swimming, 61
Float, why things do and don't, 6
Fog, cause of, 29
Fort Knox, 29
Fossils, 134
Frescoes, 12
Frog, different from toad, 146—7
Fungi, 179

G

Gagarin, Yuri, 69
Garibaldi, Guiseppe, 86—7
Geysers, 24—5
Giants, 204
Giraffes, 56
Glass, how made, 224
Golden Fleece, Order of the, 90
Goldfish, 130

Good Friday, 75
'Gothic' style of architecture, 42
Grand Canyon, The, 213
Granite, 163
Gravity, 42—3, 184
Grimm, The Brothers (Jacob and Wilhelm), 205
Gulf Stream, 166

H

Hailstones, 222
Hallowe'en (October 31), 192
Hastings, Battle of, 181
Heraldry, 95
Heredity, 211
Hermes, The winged god, 38
Hibernation, 163
Hippopotamus, 48
Horses, only one toe each foot, 9
Humming birds, 68, 150
Hurricane, different from tornado, 132

I

Ice, can it burn you?, 80
Icebergs, 88—9
Ides of March, 49
Incas, The, 166—7
Inquisition, The, 142
Insects, shining of, 116
Iron, rusting of, 99
Iron Chancellor, The (Bismarck), 25
Istanbul, 121

J

January, meaning of, 4
Joan of Arc, 96
July, meaning of, 117
June, meaning of, 98

K

Kangaroo, Australia the home of, 78
Kiwis, 100, 145
Knighthoods, 97
Knots (nautical miles), 222
Koran, The, 170
Kremlin, The, 44

L

Leather, making of, 210—11
Letters, posting of, 101
Light, speed of, 26—7
Light without heat, 9
Lightning, is it dangerous?, 78
Louis XIV, King of France ('Sun King'), 159
Louvre, The, 116
Lungs, 20, 208—9

M

Magna Carta, 105
Magnets, 150—1
Mammals, 173
    „   , intelligence of, 111
Maps (cartography), 198—9
March, meaning of, 41
Mary Queen of Scots, 38, 64
Matches, 213
May, meaning of, 79
Mercury (quicksilver), 142

Microphones, 57
Migration, 45, 165
Milky Way, The, 113
Mirages, 81
Money, 175
Moon, The, 128—9
    „   , daytime position of, 141
    „   , is it habitable?, 48
Moths, different from butterflies, 10
Motor Cars, Invention of, 54
Mould-spores, 144
Mountain, highest, 123
Mules, 147
Muscles, functions of, 63

N

Nelson's Column, 185
Nettles, stinging, 139
Newspapers, The first, 190—1
North Pole, The, 219
Notre Dame, Cathedral of, 38
November, meaning of, 193
Nursery rhymes, 131

O

Oasis, An, 182
Oceans, 89
October, meaning of, 174
Oil, origin of, 169
Opera, 11
Orchestra, An, 143
Ostrich eggs, 143
Ostriches, 100

P

Pan, The Greek god, 70
Paper, how made, 31
Parliament, oldest, 106
Passports, 30
Pearl Harbor, 216
Peat, 161
Pendulum, A, 186
Penguin, Emperor, 214
Penguins, unable to fly, 5
Penicillin, 161
Pentagon, The (Washington), 218
Pepper, 135
Periscope, 120—1
Phosphorus, 139
Photography, 22
Piano, The, 14—15
Pigeons, racing, speed of flight, 8
Pilgrim Fathers, The, 208
Pisa, Leaning Tower of, 49
Planets, The, 214
Plants, resting at night, 177
Plastics, 58
Plateaux, 30
Platinum, 128
Plimsoll, Samuel, 53
Poisons, 104
Pope, The, 114—5
Porcelain, 8
Prophets, 90
Proteins, 94
Pygmies, 52

Q

Quarries, 91
Quicksand, 183
Quicksilver (mercury), 142

R

Radar, 67
Radium, 110
Rain, causes of, 221
Rainbow, colours of, 183
Rainfall measurement of, 14
Red Cross, The, 165
Reformation, The, 72—3
Refrigerators, 206
Relativity, Theory of, 202
Renaissance, The, 47
Reptiles, 66—7
Respiration, 208—9
River water, 223
Rivers, world's longest, 194
Robin Hood, 86
Round Table, Knights of the, 176
Rubber, sources of, 55

S

St Christopher, 164
St George's Day, 74—5
St Nicholas, 215
St Patrick, Ireland's patron saint, 50
St Swithun's Day, 125
St Valentine's Day, 30—1
Salvation Army, The, 66
Salzburg and Mozart, 148
Sand, component parts of, 13
Satellites, artificial, 197
Sea, saltness of, 103
Seahorses, 93
Seashells, 140
Semaphore code, 37
Senses, human, 50, 123, 191
September, meaning of, 155
Seven Wonders of the World, 152—3
Shakespeare, William, 49, 74—5
Sheep, unable to rise if fallen over, 220
Shooting stars, 190
Shrove Tuesday, 44
Siegfried, 180
Silk, 87
Skin, how it 'breathes', 26
Skunks, 227
Sky, why it is blue, 7
Sleep, why we need, 46—7
Smell, sense of, 191
Smoke, 19
Snakes, movement of, 32
    „   , tongues of, 122
Sneezing, 114
Snowflakes, 96
Soap, 92
Soil, 115
SOS signal, 103
South Pole, first man to reach, 68—9
Spas, 229
Speech, 91
Spiders, webs of, 118, 229
Stalactites and Stalagmites, 223
Stars, daytime position of, 145
    „   , too many to count, 17
Steam, visible and invisible, 58, 188
Steam engine, invention of, 111
Stonehenge, 224—5
Sun, The, at night, 108
    „   , composition of, 64—5
Swordfish, 39

T

Tails, why animals have, 18—19

Taste, sense of, 123
Telephone, invention of, 34, 217
  „   , working of, 216—7
Television, how it works, 156—7
Thanksgiving Day, U.S.A., 208
Thistle, as emblem of Scotland, 16
Thunderbolts, 195
Tides, 129
Toad, different from frog, 146—7
Tornado, different from hurricane, 132
Tortoises and turtles, differences, 28
Trees, evergreen, 141, 225
  „   , shedding of leaves, 103
Trojan Horse of Troy, 71
Turtles and tortoises, differences, 28

U

United Nations Organisation, 187
United States, first president of, 36—7
University, oldest European, 56

Uranium, 39

V

Vaccination, 207
Vatican, The, 20—1
Venice, 135
Versailles, 151, 159
Victoria, Queen, 110
Vikings, The, 15, 133
Vitamins, 82
Volcanos, 137
Vultures, 63, 220—1

W

Wasp, different from bee, 217
Water, composition of, 58
  „   , pull of gravity on, 42—3
Water taps, working of, 35
Waterloo, Battle of, 108—9

Waves, 167
Weather forecasts, 189
Week days, meaning of, 107
Westminster Abbey, 32—3, 203
Whale, blue, largest living animal, 69
Whales, mammals not fish, 6
White House, The (Washington), 200
Windmills, 59
Woodpeckers, 166
Wright Brothers (Orville and Wilbur), 197
Writing, beginnings of, 127

X

X-rays, 61

Z

Zebras' stripes, 230
Zoos, 109

First published 1968
Fourteenth impression 1983
Published by THE HAMLYN PUBLISHING GROUP LIMITED
London · New York · Sydney · Toronto
Astronaut House, Feltham, Middlesex, England
© 1968 by The Hamlyn Publishing Group Limited
ISBN 0 601 08749 6
Printed in Czechoslovakia
51073/14